Advanced

*M*asterclass

CAE

Workbook

Tricia Aspinall

Annette Capel

OXFORD

UNIVERSITY PRESS

Oxford University Press, Great Clarendon Street, Oxford OX2 6DP

Oxford   New York
Athens   Auckland   Bangkok   Bogotá
Buenos Aires   Calcutta   Cape Town   Chennai
Dar es Salaam   Delhi   Florence   Hong Kong
Istanbul   Karachi   Kuala Lumpur   Madrid
Melbourne   Mexico City   Mumbai   Nairobi
Paris   São Paulo   Singapore   Taipei   Tokyo
Toronto   Warsaw

and associated companies in
Berlin   Ibadan

OXFORD and OXFORD ENGLISH
are trade marks of Oxford University Press

ISBN   0 19 4534294 (with key)
        0 19 4534308 (without key)

© Oxford University Press 1999

First published 1999
Second impression 2000

No unauthorized photocopying

Acknowledgements

The authors and publisher are grateful to those who have given
permission to reproduce the following extracts and adaptations of
copyright material:

p4 'I bought her a mobile phone to make sure she was safe'
by Anna Fenton. Appeared in *Woman's Own* magazine,
15 September 1997.
p8 'Running the killer desert' appeared in *Focus* December 1997
edition, and is reproduced by permission of Gruner & Jahr (U.K.)
Partners.
p10 Aromatherapy article by Mary Comber appeared in *Health &
Fitness* magazine, November 1997.
p15 'The Second-time saga' by Helena Fraser, appeared in *She
Magazine*, February 1992 © *She Magazine*, The National Magazine
Company.
p16 'The imprint of Atlantis' by David Furlong, appeared in
Kindred Spirit issue 41 (Winter 1997/98). *Kindred Spirit*, Foxhole,
Dartington, Totnes, Devon TQ9 6ED. Tel: +44 1803 866686,
Fax: +44 1803 866591. Subscription (UK) £12.00 (4 issues).
p21 'Full-time pastime' appeared in *The Economist*, 22 February
1997 issue.
p22 'Peak Performance' by Lisa Sykes appeared in *The Royal
Geographical Society Magazine*, June 1997.
p27 'Simon show suffers sound of silence' by Martin Kettle,
7 March 1998 © *The Guardian*.

p28 'Review soundings' appeared in *AN Visual Arts* magazine,
March 1998 edition.
p32 'Putting classroom before catwalk' by Clare Longrigg,
3 January 1997 © *The Guardian*.
p35 'So, I'm blind. Why shouldn't I be a BBC television director?'
by Louise Jury. Appeared in *The Independent* 21 February 1998.
p38 'The natural traveller' by Guy Marks. Appeared in
Wanderlust magazine, June/July 1997 edition.
p42 'Witness: Up the tube' by Roy Kerridge. Appeared in
Prospect magazine 4 Bedford Square, London WC1B 3RA, June
1997 issue.
p44 'Playing with fire' by Beth Nicholls. Appeared in *Wanderlust*
magazine, June/July 1997 edition.
p46 'Serving Petworth' by Diana Owen, appeared in *The National
Trust Magazine*, Summer 1997 issue © Dr. Diana Owen/*The
National Trust Magazine* 1997.
p49 'A spiritual journey' by Andrew Stevenson appeared in *The
Royal Geographical Society Magazine*, June 1997.
p50 'Wax, sunlight and X-rays' by Carole Harrison, appeared in
Nursing Times, 28 May 1997 issue.
p54 'The social effects of chronic arthritis' by Martin Leach,
appeared in *Nursing Times*, 28 May 1997 issue.
p56 'The Alien Half-Century' by Michael Harrington, 7 June 1997.
Reproduced from *The Spectator*.
p58 'Life in their hands' by Juliet Hindell, appeared in *BBC
English Magazine*, June 1997 edition.
p62 'Garbage in, garbage out' appeared in *The Economist*, 7 June
1997 issue.
p66 'Household management' appeared in *The Economist*,
17 January 1998 issue.
p68 'When a juror's the accused' by Christopher Reed, 20 May
1997 © *The Guardian*.
p74 'When silicon Saturday comes' appeared in *Focus* November
1997 edition, and is reproduced by permission of Gruner & Jahr
(U.K.) Partners.
p76 'Urban planning in the information society' by Stephen
Graham. Appeared in *Town and Country Planning* magazine,
November 1997.
p78 'I'm not a number, I'm a free shopper' by Lisa Buckingham
and Roger Cowe, 7 March 1998 © *The Guardian*.

Although every effort has been made to trace and contact
copyright holders before publication, this has not always been
possible. We apologize for any apparent infringement of
copyright and if notified, the publisher will be pleased to rectify
any errors or omissions at the earliest opportunity.

The publishers would like to thank the following for permission to
reproduce photographs:

Bob Battersby p12; Chris Bonington Photo Library p22; Cairn
Gallery, Nailsworth p29; Castlefield Gallery, Manchester p28;
Explorer p8; S & R Greenhill p72; Robert Harding Picture Library
pp4c, 16, 22 l, 62; Hutchison Library p49; Rob Judges p4a,b;
Japanese Tourist Office p44; Kobal Collection p30; London
Transport p42; Jonathan Markson Tennis Centres p11a,b; Mary
Evans Picture Library p60; National Trust p47; News International
Syndication p35; Red Orb/Broderbund p31; Rex pp27, 32, 33;
Science Photo Library pp19, 20, 38, 74, 75; Stock Market pp11c, 50,
56; Stockshot p21.

Illustrations by:

David Eaton p102; Alan Nanson pp 48, 77; Harry Venning pp 13,
40, 55, 64, 73

Design by Linda Reed & Associates

Contents

1 Loud and Clear

Reading

1 Read the whole of this text about mobile phones quickly, timing yourself as you read. Find out who bought each phone and decide who pays the bills.

These days it seems that every other teenager is walking down the street with a mobile phone glued to their ear. Here, mothers and daughters say what a mobile means to them.

Barbara (47)

'I sometimes worry that the mobile will get passed around and I'll run up a huge bill without even realizing it. That hasn't happened yet – so many of Louisa's friends have got their own anyway. They've all got used to them now, but they were very much toys to begin with. Teenagers seem to need constant communication and when the phone rings as they're walking down the street, they think it's very glamorous.'

Daughter Louisa (17)

'I was delighted when I got it but scared of taking it out in case it got pinched. I always call Mum if I'm late, and I feel much more confident with it. Out of all my friends, only about five haven't got one. It's handy – once a friend of mine had a serious medical problem and it meant we could get help quickly.'

Josée

'Vanessa's dad Terence and I were worried about keeping track of her when she was out with friends. Her safety was a big concern, especially living in London. Although I never thought I'd say it, I've come round to the idea of teenagers having them, as long as their use is strictly limited. Vanessa is not allowed to take it to school and she pays the bills out of her savings. Calls are free at weekends so she's able to have a good gossip to her mates then.'

Daughter Vanessa (15)

'My phone was an early 15th birthday present. It's a real security blanket, especially if I'm out late. I never take it to school although loads of girls do – the teachers get furious when they ring in class. My parents were dead against it at first, but when they realized it wasn't a status symbol, they agreed.'

330 words

2 Now read the text again and match these statements to the four people.

1 She can chat to her friends without it costing a fortune. — *Josée*

2 I worry about not being in control of it. — *Barbara*

3 I feel safer having it with me at night. — *Vanessa*

4 We didn't want her to have one to begin with. — *Vanessa*

5 Teenagers see having a mobile phone as a status symbol. — *barbara*

6 We wanted to know where she was at any time. — *Josée*

7 I worried about it being stolen at first. — *Louisa*

8 A mobile phone is useful in an emergency. — *Josée*

3 The text is in informal spoken English. Find these words and phrases in the text and then give more formal equivalents. An example is given.

0	run up	*accumulate*
1	pinched	*steal*
2	handy	*useful*
3	gossip	*slander, rumour (glamorous)*
4	mates	*colleagues*
5	loads of	*plenty*
6	dead against	*oppose*

4 Vanessa describes her mobile phone as a real *security blanket*, something that gives her a feeling of safety. The word 'blanket' can be a noun, an adjective or a verb. Say which part of speech it is in each of these examples and explain their meaning.

1 A layer of mist blanketed the hills and it was impossible to find our way.

2 There was blanket coverage of the scandal in the press.

3 Freddy's such a wet blanket – he wouldn't even come for a drink with us last night.

4 Many airlines now enforce a <u>blanket</u> ban on smoking. *global*

5 They encountered a blanket of silence and endless staring faces when they entered the room.

Vocabulary

While using this course, keep a separate notebook for vocabulary and try to look back at it regularly. Write down the vocabulary you learn in ways that are meaningful to you.

Here are some ideas for recording vocabulary, based on the content of Unit 1.

1 **Related parts of speech.** Use a dictionary to complete these sets of related words. Remember that the related forms may not be consecutive entries.

NOUN	ADJECTIVE	VERB
evasion	evasive	*evade*
restraint	*restrainable*	*restrain*
misinterpretation		misinterpret
distraction	*distracted*	*distract*
interruption	*interruptible*	interrupt
strategy	*strategic*	*strategize*
jerkiness	jerky	*jerk*
evaluation	*evaluative*	evaluate

2 **Meaning clouds.** Think about the meaning of the words below and put three related words into each meaning cloud. Then choose a description that matches your choice.

<u>outstanding</u> <u>unpleasant</u> <u>pitfall</u> <u>harsh</u> <u>distrust</u> <u>effective</u> <u>explain</u> distasteful <u>justify</u> <u>suspicion</u> efficient <u>snag</u> cynicism <u>nuisance</u> <u>convince</u>

a disadvantage or problem

b describing qualities

c doubt

d describing something bad

e give reasons for

outstanding, effective, efficient (b)

suspicion, distrust, harsh (c)

snag, pitfall, nuisance (a)

nuisance, cynicism, unpleasant (d) distasteful

convince, explain, justify (e)

3 Collocation. Look at dictionary examples to find some frequent collocates for words you have learnt. For example, the adjective *harsh* is often used with the following nouns:

harsh weather
a *harsh* voice
a *harsh* judgement
harsh facts / the *harsh* truth

Now write down some noun collocates for each of these adjectives.

a high-tech   _technology_
b monotonous   _monotone_
c tailor-made   _tailor_
d far-reaching   _____
e direct   _direction_
f tactless   _tact_

4 Extension. Unit 1 looked at compound adjectives ending in *-ing*, for example, *hard-hitting*. Many compound adjectives end with *-ed*. Add any you know to this list.

big-headed   _hard_-headed
                 _____-headed
open-minded   _narrow_-minded
                 broad-minded
stony-faced   _two_-faced
                 _____-faced
short-tempered   _bad_-tempered
                 _?_-tempered
light-hearted   _____-hearted
                 _____-hearted

5 Crosswords. After a lesson, record new words in simple crosswords. Then write some simple definitions and try them on your classmates! Write the definitions for the words in this crossword.

```
                    ¹J
 ²C O M M U N I C A T I O N
  Y                 R
  N      ³F I D G E T
  I                 O
  C                 N
  I
 ⁴S E N T I M E N T A L
  M
```

6 Register. Remember to note down any usage restrictions when you list new vocabulary and record informal and more formal equivalents together.

Suggest phrasal verbs which have a similar meaning to these verbs. An example is given.

0 wait   _**hang on**_
1 avoid   _____
2 defer   _____
3 reprimand _____
4 increase   _go up_
5 specify   _____

Writing

Choose suitable words to complete this note to a friend. The words come from the Vocabulary Resource (1 Apologizing) and from Unit 1 itself.

excuses   unconvincing   let   tactless   guilty
upset   harsh   splendid   pretend   sorry

Dear Kate

I am so (1)_ Sorry _ that I forgot to come to your wedding last week. I feel really (2)_ guilty _ about it, particularly as you sent me such a (3)_ splendid _ invitation. I can't give any (4)_ excuses _ for this (5)_ tactless _ behaviour – even if I (6)_ pretend _ to you that I am busy at work, I know you will find this (7)_ unconvincing _ as a reason. The (8)_ harsh _ reality is that I've (9)_ let _ you down. I can only tell you again how (10)_ upset _ I feel and hope that you'll forgive me.

Love Rachel

English in Use

Part 3

In most lines of the following text, there is either a spelling or a punctuation error.
For each numbered line 1–12, write the correctly spelled words or show the correct
punctuation. Some lines are correct. The exercise begins with three examples (0).

To have and have not

In America, the Internet is seen as an assett that you must buy.

You purchase a computer put it in your home somewhere,

choose an online service, and then find a teenager to set it up

for you. But what about people who dont have the money to

buy a computer, new or used or who have no phone line in

their home? Or who are indeed homeless? According to a

recent survey, the "have-nots are logging on to the Internet in

record numbers. They are making use of what the survey calls

"alternative points of access", including schools, churchs and

other public sites. The situation is at varience with a common

belief that the Internet is increasing the gap between the rich

and poor. The unemployed are flocking to public librairies

to explore job banks online, while people on welfare are using

free online access to learn about which goverment services

might be available to them. Given this could there actually be

an advantage to "not-having"?

0	_asset_
0	_computer, put_
0	✓
1	dont
2	_____
3	_____
4	_____
5	_____
6	churches
7	_____
8	Internet
9	_____
10	_____
11	_____
12	_____

Structure

Read the following sets of sentences carefully and mark the odd one out in each case.
Explain your choice.

1 a Have you been studying English for a long
      time?
   b Did you study English for a long time?
   c Have you studied English for a long time?
   Did you study English for a long time?

2 a Paul used to have a mobile phone.
   b Paul used his mobile phone to call the office.
   c Paul used to call the office on his mobile phone.
   Paul used his mobile phone to

3 a You ought to take notice of her advice.
   b You'd do well to take notice of her advice.
   c You did well to take notice of her advice.
   You did well to take notice of

4 a I hope you won't butt in while I'm speaking.
   b I wish you wouldn't butt in while I'm
      speaking.
   c If only you wouldn't butt in while I'm
      speaking.
   If only you

5 a The government has misled the public about
      tax cuts.
   b The government is said to have misled the
      public about tax cuts.
   c The public have been misled by the
      government about tax cuts.
   The government is said to have

Fighting Fit

Reading

1 Read this article quickly, ignoring the missing headings. Why does Roland Somogyvary's name appear twice in the *Guinness Book of Records*?

Running the killer desert

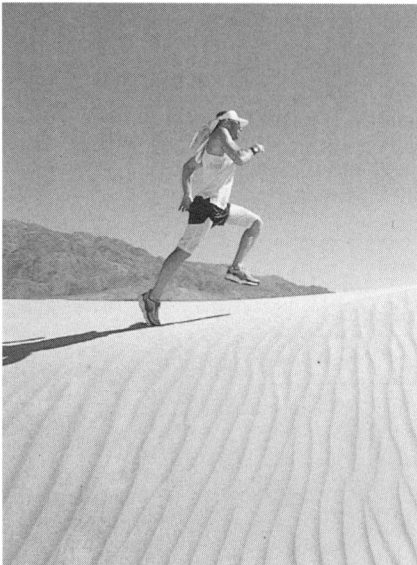

(0) __H__

Roland Somogyvary is a Frenchman who relishes gruelling, record-breaking runs. He won an entry in the 1989 *Guinness Book of Records* for covering 600km from Las Vegas to Phoenix in only six days. On his return to France, a friend asked: "Why not do Death Valley?" Why not indeed? No one had crossed it in less than five days, but Roland knew he could do a lot better, if he didn't stop.

(1)_____

Roland began training more or less immediately, but it took a full eight years for his plans to come to fruition. Twice, the attempt was called off at the last minute, but

in 1997, Roland gave up his job in a shop and devoted himself full-time to endurance running. He was determined to see the project through and picked July 19, which was likely to be the hottest day of the year, as his target date. What was his reason? "The idea was that no one could follow and do it any better. It would just be me and my will to run it in one go." California's Death Valley has an extremely harsh climate, with temperatures soaring above 50°C. As part of his preparation, Roland consulted a nutritionist for advice on what sort of diet his body would require during such a run. The nutritionist was pessimistic about Roland's chances in the fierce heat, and predicted that he would be forced to give up within five hours.

(2)_____

But this grim warning came too late – there was no way Roland would chicken out now. Off he flew to California, accompanied by his two brothers, André and Jean-Claude, who were going to keep up with him on mountain bikes; a doctor, who would try to ensure Roland didn't keel over too early; and a logistics man, who would drive the doctor and his equipment, as well as 300 litres of water and liquid food. Together, they had planned the route meticulously. Roland would run at a speed of between 5 and 9 km/h, depending on the terrain and the temperature. He'd slow down every 15 minutes to gulp down some food, and take very brief stops every hour for a change of T-shirt or running shoes. Sun-block would be put on at 30-minute intervals, to protect him from the sun's killer rays.

(3)_____

When they reached the starting point, conditions were even worse than they had expected, with a searing ground temperature of 93°C. The Death Valley Rangers tried to persuade Roland not to go and reckoned

that this mad Frenchman would collapse within three hours. Nevertheless, at five o'clock on the sweltering afternoon of 19 July, Roland set off. There would be no real rest now for 170km. He recounts: "I had truly prepared myself for sheer hell, but the reality was still a slap in the face." At least he didn't have to cope with excess sweating: it was so scorching that the beads of moisture dried on his body as soon as they appeared!

(4)_____

During the night, Roland experienced hallucinations, but he managed to keep going and completed 60km. As a spectacular dawn bled into the sky, Roland faced a further challenge: over the next 60km he would go from 85m below sea level to an altitude of 1500m. He had now been running for 14 hours, and the heat hadn't once dropped below 45°C. It was at this point that the back-up car broke down. Both the driver and the doctor had to stay behind to sort it out, leaving Roland and his brothers to press on for over an hour without a single drop of water. Roland remembers feeling the strain: "I'd entered the 'danger zone', but somehow my legs kept going. With each step, though, I had the impression I was hitting a wall."

(5)_____

It was now time to take on Strawberry Pass, where Roland would encounter the roughest terrain of the entire run and a blistering temperature of 55°C. Somehow he made it. Wild with fatigue, seriously dehydrated, and having run for a full 28 hours, Roland eventually came to a very thankful halt. "I had dreamt about that moment for eight years," he says. "There were initial set-backs, but we got through Death Valley – and survived." Roland Somogyvary now has two entries in the *Guinness Book of Records*.

⏱ **750 words**

2 Decide on the best headings for 1–5, choosing from A–H. An example is given.

A The back-up contingent

B Facing up to injury

C The end of the line

D Prepared for anything

E Long-distance loneliness

F An uphill struggle

G A fiery welcome

H Taking up the challenge

3 The article contains a number of words to describe the intense heat. How many can you find?

4 These phrasal verbs come from the article. Match them to meanings 1–8.

a	call off	1	withdraw
b	see through	2	continue
c	chicken out	3	swallow quickly
d	keep up with	4	deal with
e	keel over	5	complete successfully
f	gulp down	6	cancel
g	sort out	7	move at the same speed as
h	press on	8	faint

Can you find eight more phrasal verbs in the article?

Structure

1 Complete these sentences about Roland Somogyvary, choosing a suitable modal verb.

a Roland _____ really enjoy long-distance running.

b A friend of his suggested he _____ run through Death Valley.

c Roland _____ wait eight years for the chance to fulfil his ambition.

d He chose July 19 so that no one else _____ ever better his achievement.

e The nutritionist thought that Roland _____ possibly keep going for more than five hours.

f Roland and his team _____ worked very hard at the planning stage.

g The Death Valley Rangers believed that Roland _____ gone ahead with the run.

h During the run, Roland _____ stop while he was taking food and water.

i Because of its terrain, Strawberry Pass _____ been more difficult to run through.

j Roland felt exhausted at the end, and he _____ been in pain too. We don't know.

2 Complete these pairs of sentences and explain the differences in meaning between the two modals.

a You mustn't eat that chocolate –

It's not yours! _____

You shouldn't have any more wine –

_____

b Fitness centres must be doing really good business –

_____

Fitness centres ought to charge a bit less –

_____

c I didn't need to buy a ticket in advance –

_____

I should have reserved a seat –

_____

d That holiday must have cost a fortune –

_____

That holiday needn't have cost so much –

_____

e It couldn't have been John you saw in town –

_____

It might have been John you saw in town –

_____

Vocabulary

For questions 1–15, read the text below and then decide which word,
A, B, C or D, best fits each space. An example is given.

Luxurious rose-scented soaps, a (0)____ mint after dinner – you needn't have (1)____ aromatherapy to understand the therapeutic powers of essential oils. These magical liquids, (2)____ from a range of aromatic plants, offer a truly holistic therapy, because they work on both body and (3)____ .

When you put (4)____ oils in your evening bath to help you to relax, you are recreating rituals that are thousands of years old. Hippocrates (5)____ that the secret of health was an aromatic bath and scented massage every day. Cleopatra bathed in jasmine, while other Egyptians blended oils to (6)____ as medicines. In Shakespearian Britain, women spread rosemary and lavender on floors to (7)____ and purify rooms.

Now it has been (8)____ in various scientific studies that many of these essential oils have powerful antiseptic and anti-bacterial uses. A recent Australian report found that tea tree oil was the only (9)____ to kill all the types of antibiotic-resistant bacteria tested. Therapists know that tea tree oil can (10)____ minor wounds. It seems that every essential oil (11)____ of hundreds of chemicals, all with potential healing and medicinal properties. When an oil is (12)____ , these chemicals enter the body's system and bloodstream.

Compared to drugs, the oils' (13)____ are fairly weak, but this in itself makes the oils safe (14)____ . For this reason, aromatherapy is often introduced as treatment (15)____ conventional medicine, to complement mainstream medical practices.

⏱ **250 words**

0	A <u>strong</u>	B spicy	C hot	D sharp
1	A experimented	B tasted	C tried	D checked
2	A extracted	B pulled	C brought	D cut
3	A brain	B head	C thinking	D mind
4	A stimulating	B soothing	C sentimental	D soft
5	A claimed	B communicated	C evaluated	D expressed
6	A make	B use	C do	D set
7	A wash	B remove	C destroy	D cleanse
8	A appeared	B presented	C shown	D pointed
9	A substance	B matter	C element	D material
10	A mend	B treat	C care	D attend
11	A contains	B consists	C comprises	D composes
12	A inhaled	B drawn	C breathed	D gulped
13	A results	B conclusions	C effects	D issues
14	A reliefs	B recipes	C repairs	D remedies
15	A between	B alongside	C next	D together

Writing

In Part 1 of the Writing paper, you must avoid lifting words and phrases that appear in the question. Look at the advertisement for tennis holidays and the notes a friend has made on it. Then read the extract from the friend's letter. Reword the underlined phrases in the letter, choosing adjectives from the Vocabulary Resource (6.3) where appropriate and adding words of your own. Then make other improvements to the letter – for example, the writer has used *very* six times – try different words for variety!

ACE Tennis Holidays

Yes! **Relax** at the best tennis centre in Europe – lots of tennis, and watersports too!

None – v. disappointing

- Full programme of coaching and tournaments *Not much – did own thing*
- Large villas, all fully-furnished and well-equipped *v. large but v. basic*
- Accommodation set in beautiful surroundings *Yes, beautiful*
- Quiet beaches within easy reach *Quiet but diff. to get to*
- Close to airport, motorway and rail connections *Not exactly…*

So you're thinking of going on an Ace holiday? I had a good time in the end, but be warned, the advert isn't very accurate. Let me tell you a bit more about my experience.

You can certainly <u>relax</u> – there was <u>not much of a tennis programme</u> when I went. This didn't matter, in fact, because I went with three other people and we were able to <u>do our own thing</u>. But as for <u>watersports, there were none</u>. This was very disappointing because one of the reasons I chose this holiday was to learn to windsurf.

I did stay in a large villa – it was <u>very large</u>, in fact. Four of us were in this six-bedroomed villa, but <u>it wasn't well-equipped and it was very basic</u>. The villa <u>was set in very beautiful surroundings</u> though.

We did find some <u>quiet beaches</u> but they were <u>very difficult to get to</u>. As we used to go to the beach after a full morning's tennis, we needed to have at least one beach <u>within easy reach</u>.

Finally, I must tell you that it took us four hours to get from the airport, so the centre was <u>not exactly close to it</u>.

3 Getting to Know You

Reading

1 Read through this article and choose the best title, a, b or c.

a   Why I prefer to be a single mother

b   My partner behaves like a child

c   Second marriages don't work

Whenever people ask how many children I've got, I say three: Adam, 10, and Paul, 8, from my first marriage – and 29-year-old Brian, the biggest kid of all! He's been like that since we met, though I only picked up on it later. I'd been single for two years and when I first met him, I thought he was an idiot. I mean, he wore even weirder clothes then, and played practical jokes on people – mind you, he still does, though I don't find it offensive myself.

As I got to know Brian better, I discovered just how juvenile he is. Generally, I don't mind what he does, unless it affects Adam or Paul. One day he got told off in a toy shop for playing with the goods – and I've never forgotten how he sulked when I refused to buy him a water pistol! Everything in the house has been taken to bits by him at some time or other, including the boys' computer, which is really unacceptable. He's driven me mad at times playing his guitar and he won't get his hair cut because he fancies himself as a rock star, but I know how much it means to him so I leave well alone.

He hasn't got a steady job and although he started a computer course, he dropped out recently, so I've been keeping us afloat with my teaching. I used to give him £20 a week pocket money, but I've stopped that. It's not the money in itself, but while he had it, he didn't need to worry about earning for himself. It's strange living with such a big kid – my first husband, Steve, had always taken responsibility for things, but marriage to Brian has meant the complete opposite.

My friends wonder what I'm doing with him, but our relationship really does work. Before we met, I went out with someone who had a regular job and did his share of the housework, but he bored me to tears! That's what's different about Brian, the fun. If there was ever a crisis, I'm sure he would be there for me, too. I work with children who have emotional and behavioural problems, so I'm surrounded by kids all the time. Brian is just another one to look after. And although I don't enjoy being a mother figure, I came to terms with it a long time ago.

Brian replies:

"I've always fooled around, but then there's nothing wrong with having a good time, is there? I think everyone should keep the child alive in them. Don't all men like playing with toys? Secretly, I think Helen likes looking after me, even though she would deny this."

Counsellor Sarah Wilson comments:

Relationship imbalance like this is common. A lot of couples have one partner who's the carer, and that's fine if they're happy in the role. But problems start if the carer gets fed up and decides it's time for an adult-to-adult relationship. Sometimes they become embarrassed by their partner, or grow tired of taking all the responsibility. But once behaviour patterns are set, no one can change overnight. The only way forward is for both sides to compromise.

535 words

2 Now answer questions 1–6, underlining the parts of the article which give you the answers.

1 Helen wasn't impressed by Brian when they first met because she

   A found his behaviour childish.
   B thought he was badly-dressed.
   C reacted against his tactlessness.
   D felt he was too light-hearted.

2 What does Helen most dislike about Brian?

   A his long hair
   B his childish behaviour in public places
   C his moodiness
   D his interference with her boys' things

3 Why has Helen stopped giving Brian pocket money?

   A He has completed his computer course.
   B She can't afford to continue paying it.
   C He doesn't need the money now.
   D She wants him to look for a job.

4 Why does Helen think their relationship is successful?

   A She enjoys her dominant role.
   B She is entertained by Brian.
   C She finds Brian supportive.
   D She can look after everyone.

5 What does Brian say about himself?

   A He should be allowed to enjoy life.
   B He has no desire to have children.
   C He knows what is best for Helen.
   D He is no different from other men.

6 Why can relationship imbalance cause problems?

   A It is impossible to change roles quickly.
   B It is embarrassing for the less dominant one.
   C It is too demanding on the carer.
   D It is difficult to reach a compromise.

3 Find these phrases in the article and match them to the best meanings, choosing from 1–6. Then find phrases in the article for the two extra meanings.

a picked up on   _____

b played practical jokes on   _____

c taken to bits   _____

d dropped out   _____

1 learned to accept
2 left early
3 discovered
4 tricked
5 behaved irresponsibly
6 dismantled

4 The prefixes used in 5 and 6 above are negative in meaning. Use negative prefixes with these words and fit them into the sentences about Brian. There is one extra word that you don't need.

offensive   mature   suitable   intelligent
incentive   employment

a Though 29, Brian is basically very

   _____ .

b There is nothing to suggest that he is

   _____ , though he does appear to be

   rather silly!

c Giving Brian pocket money was a

   _____ to his finding work.

d Helen is tolerant of Brian's behaviour, finding it

   _____ on the whole.

e Helen's friends think Brian is _____

   for her.

Vocabulary

1 Read the following short text, where a personnel advisor talks about job interviews. Then look at gaps 1–8 and decide what part of speech is required in each. Make suitable words from the ones given in capital letters, remembering to add negative prefixes where necessary.

> I've heard of really unusual interviews, where the interviewer starts by lying down on the floor, and then waits for the person's (0)__*reaction*__ to his behaviour. Apparently, the successful (1)_____ is the one who gets down on the floor and does the same thing! First (2)_____ mean a lot to interviewers, which can be very (3)_____. In fact, one consultant claims that words contribute a (4)_____ tiny 7% of the total message a person communicates, with tone of voice making up a further 38%. The rest is non-verbal – body language, (5)_____ expression and clothes. You look for signs that show someone is being less than (6)_____: they may touch their nose or scratch their ear, or start fiddling with a collar or tie. Arms and legs are (7)_____ difficult to control when a person is trying to mask emotions. This is known as (8)_____, so, for example, if someone crosses their arms or legs, it suggests suppressed aggression.

0	ACT	5	FACE
1	APPLY	6	TRUE
2	IMPRESS	7	POSSIBLE
3	FORTUNE	8	LEAK
4	PROPORTION		

2 Look at the following examples and decide which word fits best, 'brimming', 'gushing' or 'streaming'. If necessary, check the usage of these words in a dictionary first.

a It was Toshack on the phone, _____ with gratitude as he rustled his contract.

b An eye-witness described seeing smoke _____ from one engine.

c The company is proud of its _____ order books, particularly in the aerospace division.

d Our table included the sponsor's wife, a _____ froth of a lady in an unbecoming lemon dress.

e This is a side _____ with ability and confidence.

f The authorities were unable to cope with the huge numbers of unemployed peasants _____ into the cities.

g There was blood _____ down her white nightdress.

h When you visited me, you were always _____ over with news of where you had been.

Structure

1 Complete the sentences with a suitable form of the verbs in brackets, adding negative forms where necessary.

a Unless people _____ (book) tickets already, it _____ (be) possible to attend tonight's performance.

b If Kevin _____ (tell) his mother what had happened, she _____ (sort out) the whole misunderstanding long ago.

c Even if you _____ (be) to get the job, how _____ (sell) the house in time?

d If you _____ (bring) someone else's book home, you _____ (return) it to school the next day, don't you?

e If only you _____ (behave) less childishly, you _____ (get) more cooperation from him, instead of his usual response.

f Unless he _____ (go) shopping now, there _____ (be) anything for supper.

g Even if an interviewer _____ (try) to put the candidate at ease, it _____ (be) usually still a very stressful situation.

h If you _____ (notice) that the figures were wrong, why _____ (wait) until now to tell me?

2 Read the text below about remarriage and fill in the spaces, writing one word only. An example is given.

The second-time saga

It was so simple (0) __*the*__ first time round, my main anxieties (1)_____ what dress to wear to the wedding and (2)_____ to invite. Twenty years ago, it (3)_____ occurred to me to worry about money or to contemplate what (4)_____ happen if it all fell apart.

However, this time, all (5)_____ aware of the failure rate of second marriages, and with children from our previous relationships to think about, we've prepared (6)_____ the worst, spending the last month absorbed in the (7)_____ than romantic details of wills and life assurance. I have to say (8)_____ hasn't been much fun. We've asked all sorts of morbid questions, such (9)_____ What if one of us falls under a bus? What if

(10)_____ of us do? Our main priority has been to produce wills dealing with (11)_____ possible eventuality, though this hasn't been easy.

The other nightmare scenario was splitting up. What if we decided we couldn't stand (12)_____ other within the first couple of years? The administrative answer to this was fairly simple, involving us (13)_____ signing a pre-nuptial contract, stating our intention to walk away with (14)_____ resources we had brought into the marriage. Pre-nuptial contracts have (15)_____ actual force at all in English law, but we certainly felt better after we had signed. We were at long last ready to enjoy our wedding!

Writing

Change the underlined parts of this account to make the writing more consistently formal.

1 __Mr Booth_____
2 _____
3 _____
4 _____
5 _____
6 _____
7 _____
8 _____
9 _____
10 _____
11 _____
12 _____
13 _____
14 _____

To Gilbert Booth, Headmaster of Westreach Secondary School

Dear (1) *Gilbert*

I am a pensioner and have lived opposite your school for (2)*ages*. Although I have many happy memories of former pupils, this year I have become increasingly upset and (3)*fed up with* the appalling manners of your current pupils. (4)*I can't stand it any longer*, so I am writing to you in the hope that you will (6)*sort it out*.

Before school and at lunchtimes, rebellious gangs of teenagers gather outside my front gate. They (7)*puff* cigarettes and (8)*chuck* their drinks cans and half-eaten sandwiches into my garden. (9)*I say*, the language they use is quite shocking. Why should I have to listen to torrents of rude words while I (10)*polish off* my breakfast and lunch? (11)*It's not fair, is it?*

If your school represents the younger generation of today, there's no hope for the future. (12)*Please* do something to (13)*make things better*.

(14)*Love*

Mrs Ada Smart

Can You Believe It?

Reading

1 These two photographs have something in common, according to the writer David Furlong. Read the text below to find out what this is.

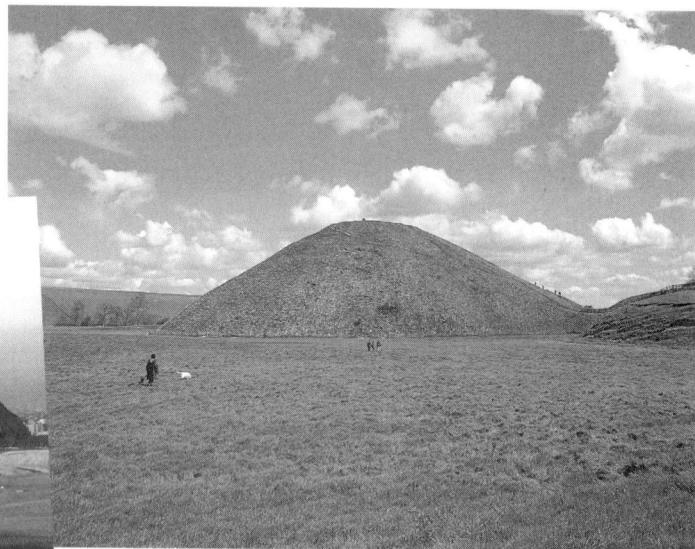

▲ Silbury Hill

◀ The Great Pyramid

THE IMPRINT OF **ATLANTIS**

*Legend has it that Atlantis was an advanced civilisation existing around 5000 years ago, which suddenly sank without trace into the Atlantic Ocean. But what if Atlantis had truly existed and its inhabitants had had time to leave before the final cataclysm? Where would they have gone? **David Furlong**, author of **The Keys to the Temple**, believes passionately in Atlantis and argues that its people ended up in Britain and Egypt. He offers his evidence in the following article.*

2 Check you understand the words in a–e below before reading the article. Match each set to an overall definition, choosing from 1–5.

a lasting legacy legend

b circumference geometric proportional ratio

c architecturally construction monument surveying

d cataclysm catastrophic doomed upheaval

e sacred spiritual

1 to do with an unavoidable event, usually harmful

2 to do with building work

3 relating to beliefs

4 mathematical terms

5 of historical significance

3 Read the first two paragraphs of the article. Then look at paragraphs A–F and decide what each one is about. Finally, sort these paragraphs into the correct order. Remember to check that each paragraph links with the one before and after it.

4 Find examples of the following in the text and decide why they have been used.

a present perfect (paragraph 1)

b past perfect (paragraph A)

c past perfect continuous (paragraph 2)

d simple past (paragraph C)

e modal with perfect infinitive (paragraph E)

f modal referring to the past (paragraph F)

IN 1975, I made the dramatic discovery that there is a massive geometric pattern of two overlapping circles in the landscape of Wiltshire. This stretches for over 27km and within the two circles lies a clue to the construction of the Great Pyramid of Egypt. It has taken me 25 years of research, with the help of a desktop computer, to be able to prove beyond doubt that this pattern exists. The two circles are of identical size, around 9.5km across. A cross-section of the Great Pyramid fits exactly within their overlapping area. Both have a number of ancient sites sitting precisely on their circumferences. Most incredibly of all, my computer calculations have shown that these circles are exactly proportional to the equatorial circumference of the earth, in the ratio of 1:666.

This article is reproduced by kind permission of *Kindred Spirit* magazine.

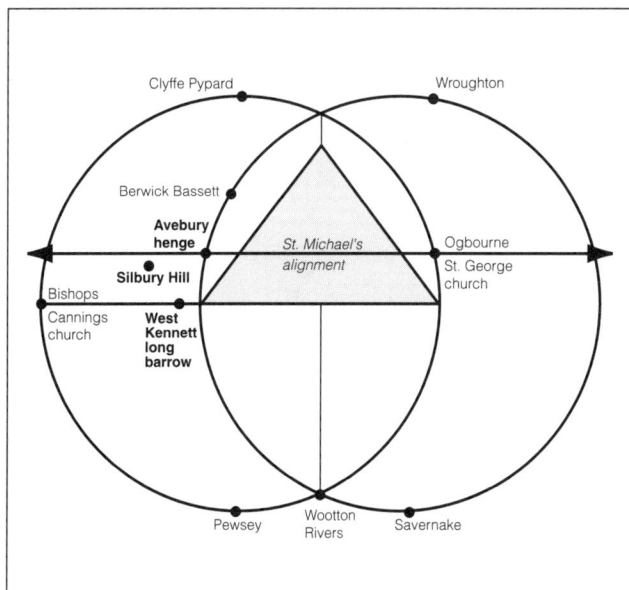

The peoples of Britain in the late Neolithic period seem to have been highly intelligent, possessing great skills in surveying, engineering, mathematics and astronomy. Architecturally, they had been building long, straight earthworks for some time, but quite suddenly, 5100 years ago, they started to construct circular patterns, such as stone circles. It is believed that the earliest phase of Stonehenge was around 3100BC and the most important circular sites in Britain were all started within 100 years or so of this date.

A

The Mayan people had therefore been exactly right in maintaining that their calendar marked a catastrophic date. Could their belief that their ancestors came from lands that were overwhelmed in some way also have been true? Despite all the research into the Atlantic sea bed, no clear evidence has emerged; no undersea kingdom has been discovered and scientists say that nothing of this sort exists on the Atlantic floor. But perhaps Atlantis was so thoroughly destroyed that nothing now remains?

B

What scientific evidence is there to support such a cataclysmic event? Surprisingly, there is a great deal, in the area of climatic change. Ice-core samples from Greenland show a significant sulphate deposit, dated at approximately 3100BC. Around the world, at the same time, there is further evidence of serious geological upheavals, for example, a dramatic rise and fall in sea level along the coast of Brittany in France and flooding in the Navajo country of the American Southwest.

C

Research in America and elsewhere has similarly shown that the pyramid shape affects the energy fields of the human body and can be used to speed up the healing process when injuries occur. I believe that the energy to be found in Wiltshire is a power that is infinitely liberating. The people from Atlantis, forced to take their knowledge into the world around them, left us this huge legacy, and their sites are once more communicating their messages to us. We only have to stop and listen.

D

This is my own belief. So let us assume that a group of Atlantean emigrés, fleeing from their doomed homeland, set foot on the shores of Britain and Egypt, bringing with them their advanced knowledge and skills in surveying and the like. In Egypt, this eventually led to the building of the Great Pyramid, while in Britain, the same expertise was used to create a vast geometric pattern in the landscape. Yet why set out these sites in geometric patterns? What was so special about the pyramid shape that it occurs both in the British landscape and as a lasting monument in Egypt?

E

This historical period is highly significant in at least two other parts of the world. The civilisation of ancient Egypt bloomed at around this time, so quickly that Egyptologists have concluded that there must have been some additional cultural influence entering Egypt. On the other side of the Atlantic, the Mayan civilisation, despite being much later (600AD), actually observed 3114BC as the starting date of their calendar. They maintained that this exact year had seen the catastrophic end of their original culture, in which their first homelands, lying somewhere to the east, had been completely destroyed.

F

During more than 25 years researching sacred sites, and through my experiences as a spiritual healer, I have been aware of a healing presence at such places. Certain sites stimulated a clear bodily sensation in me, where I would get a tingling feeling in my head and arms. For many years I could not prove that this was not a purely subjective phenomenon. However, I am now sure that something much deeper is at work. It is my belief that the ancient Atlanteans brought with them a form of healing energy, which they wove into the landscape through the geometric patterns that they established.

Structure

1 Read the text below quickly, to understand the time period involved.
Then fill in the spaces, using the verbs in brackets in a suitable tense.

I (1)_____ (never, believe) in ghosts until I (2)_____ (spend) a weekend in my friend's remote cottage in Scotland. It (3)_____ (be abandoned) by an old sheep farmer many years before this friend of mine (4)_____ (buy) it for next to nothing in 1991. He (5)_____ (promise) to invite me up there for ages, so when he finally (6)_____ (get) round to asking me, I (7)_____ (accept) his offer willingly. We (8)_____ (set) off on that fateful Friday in a downpour and the rain (9)_____ (continue) throughout our six-hour drive. By the time we (10)_____ (reach) the cottage it (11)_____ (get) dark and we only just (12)_____ (manage) to make it out in the gloom. Relieved that we (13)_____ (finally, get) there, we (14)_____ (start) to make a fire and generally make ourselves comfortable. There (15)_____ (be) no electricity of course, but we (16)_____(bring) one of those camping lamps with us, as well as some candles. Eventually we (17)_____ (settled down) and (18)_____ (enjoy) a relaxing chat by the fire when the floorboards in the room above suddenly (19)_____ (begin) to creak. At first, we (20)_____ (take) no notice, but the noise (21)_____ (become) more and more distracting and we (22)_____ (get) very anxious. In the end, I (23)_____ (decide) to go up and have a look, so I (24)_____ (light) a candle and (25)_____ (creep) up the stairs. As I (26)_____ (turn) the corner at the top, the candle (27)_____ (blow) out. I (28)_____ (feel) this inexplicable icy coldness and an unnatural presence close beside me. I (29)_____ (must, scream) because my friend (30)_____ (come) rushing up the stairs noisily. Then I (31)_____ (realize) that whatever I (32)_____ (witness) (33)_____ (be) over. At the time, my friend (34)_____ (claim) he (35)_____ (never, experience) such a phenomenon and, despite visiting the cottage frequently since, he (36)_____ (find) nothing out of the ordinary. Personally, I (37)_____ (never, want) to set foot there again and I (38)_____ (do) my best to forget the entire incident, although I am still very perplexed by it.

2 Decide which alternative is correct in these sentences.

a As a young child, Kaspar Hauser *used to / got used to* see nobody for weeks on end.

b After she got her own TV show, she became quite a celebrity and *would / was used to* be recognised everywhere she went.

c If you had spent more time with David, I'm sure you'd *get used to / be used to* his eccentric behaviour by now.

d Now that Judy's gone away to university, her room will be *used for / used to* visitors.

e So keen on creature comforts am I that I have never *been used to / got used to* sleeping in a tent.

English in Use

Part 3

There is one unnecessary word in most of the lines of this text. Write these words in the space provided. Tick any lines that are correct. Two examples are given.

The comet Hale-Bopp

Text	Line	Answer
Comets wander through deepest space. Occasionally,	0	✓
and for only a so short time, we are privileged to view	0	so ✓
this wonderful natural phenomenon as from earth. In	1	as
April 1997, the comet Hale-Bopp made out its closest	2	out ✓
approach to our sun and its appearance had caught	3	had
the attention of professional and amateur astronomers	4	✓ ✓
alike. The comet had in fact and only been discovered	5	and ✓
in the July 1995. During those April evenings, Hale-Bopp	6	✓ the
provided to us with an unforgettable sight. Night after	7	with to
night, because thanks to clear skies, this magical body	8	✓ because
was clearly visible to the naked eye, trailing its elegant,	9	✓ ✓
long dust tail across the all night sky. Though still briefly	10	all ✓
visible in early May, it has eventually disappeared that	11	✓ has
month, was heading back into the outer solar system.	12	after was
Observers around the world agreed that Hale-Bopp was	13	✓
the most complex structure they had never seen and	14	✓ never
considered themselves fortunate to have witnessed it.	15	✓

(handwritten notes above Vocabulary:) shoot up → crecer rápidamente (child, plant) / dispararse (prices) / chutarse / set off = provocar, ponerse en camino / hacer estallar

Vocabulary

Combine the following verbs and particles to make phrasal verbs, some of which have come up in this unit. Use a dictionary to check any you are unsure about. Then use some of the phrasal verbs in the sentences below.

set	**up**	shoot
end	**off**	seep *filtrarse, rezumar*
wear	**out**	speed

a Although they tried to keep the story out of the public eye, the news __seep out__ eventually.

b When the pain had still not __wear off__ after three days, Sally consulted a doctor about her injury.

c It can take a long time to __set up__ a new business.

d The police __sped off__ in pursuit of the stolen car. *búsqueda*

e Skiing off-piste is dangerous, as it can __set off__ an avalanche.

f The weary travellers __ended up__ in a deserted cabin, where they spent an uncomfortable night. *exhausted*

g Jimmy surprised us by __shooting out__ from behind a tree.

h My boots had completely __worn out__, so I bought some new ones.

Writing

Below is the opening paragraph of another entry to the competition on famous people from the past (see page 56 of the Student's Book). Make the changes suggested, in order to improve the originality and clarity of the piece. Then complete the entry, using the paragraph plan and notes provided.

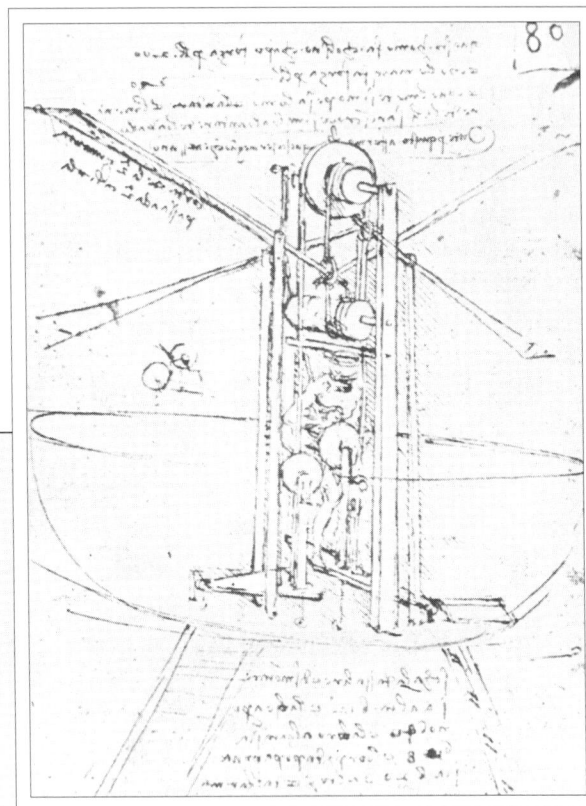

Rework opening sentence to make an impact, and use a different adjective here – he was better than good! Start sentence with a noun phrase? 'A...painter,'

Leonardo da Vinci was a <u>good</u> painter, who lived during the Renaissance period. It would be <u>nice</u> to meet him, not just because of his <u>painting</u> skills but also because he was a great scholar, exploring virtually every area of science.

use 'privilege'

make adjective from 'art'

start sentence with topic adverb ⟨ He was far ahead of his time, even designing flying machines. I would like to ask him about these designs and find out <u>what</u> he had in mind. If he shared his scientific knowledge with me, it would <u>help me</u> in my own studies.

use 'precisely'?

stronger!

Second paragraph:
Also ask about art – Mona Lisa! Who? Why smiling? His favourite painting?

Third paragraph:
Ask about his life – left Florence for Milan in 1482 (18 years there). Missed Florence? When and where happiest?

Ending:
Reinforce reason for meeting him – most creative man ever

5 All Walks of Life

English in Use

Part 3

In most lines of the following text, there is **either** a spelling **or** a punctuation error. For each numbered line 1–12, write the correctly spelled words or show the correct punctuation, Some lines are correct. The exercise begins with three examples.

FULL-TIME PASTIME

What is a ski bum?
Our correspondent scours the Rockies for the answer.

Among the skier packed on the cable car heading to the summit	0	*skiers*
of Snowbird is a particularly unkempt specimen. His eyes	0	✓
are sunken behind his ski-goggles an untidy beard flows	0	*goggles; an*
down his chest. 'I'm a lifer', he says proudly. At first you take	1	
him to mean that he is a escaped convict. What he means to say	2	
is that he has bought Snowbirds lifetime ski pass at the price of a	3	
small car. His only wish is to remain healthy enough to brake even	4	
on the deal. He skies almost every day of the season. A true ski bum	5	
welcomes the autism that comes with repitition. He, or, nowadays, just	6	
as often, she lives only in the moment, shutting out the world and	7	
concentrating on the next carved turn. It is easy enough to spot them	8	
sking on the mountain. Above all, the ski bum must possess the	9	
discipline to ski hard all day, every day. He aims all ways to be the	10	
first on and the last of the mountains. He does not let the weather or his	11	
physical, financial or emotional state intefer. A ski bum values the	12	
bum element and ski instructors, in particular, are viewed as a separate		
and somewhat peculiar species.		

Reading

1 Quickly read through the first paragraph and find out what Alan Hinkes is planning to do.

2 Skim through the multiple-choice questions before reading the rest of the text. You do not need to read the options at this stage.

3 Now read the text carefully and answer questions 1–6.

Peak Performance

The Alpine Club in London has all the ambience and bonhomie of a country pub, where the regulars have been coming for years to chew the fat over great climbs. Many mountaineers have spoken here before; this particular evening, the floor is given over to Alan Hinkes, who is introduced by the club's president, Sir Chris Bonington. Hinkes is speaking before he sets off on his attempt to become the first Briton to climb all 14 of the world's highest peaks over 8000 metres. While five men have already achieved this feat, he will be the first to climb six within a year.

Even his good friends only give him 100:1 odds of achieving this goal, says Bonington, "his less good friends 1000:1". But Hinkes refuses to even listen to such doubting talk. It is not a case of "if" he manages to achieve his final ascent (Nepal's Anapurna I) but, he says, "when".

It was during his first attempt at an "8000er" in the Himalayas in 1987 that he first thought about attempting "the 14", as the world's 14 highest peaks are known in mountaineering circles.

Over the next 10 years, Hinkes gradually climbed another seven of the 8000ers. Then followed three years during which he made three attempts on the world's hardest mountain, Pakistan's 8611-metre-high K2.

"K2 is not much lower than Everest", explains Hinkes, "so you have all the same altitude problems". It is also much more difficult to climb, he adds. "In 93 I had to retreat to help a guy down who was in a really bad way, then the next year I got very near the top but wasn't happy with the snow conditions – I thought it might avalanche".

Hinkes' maxim, which he repeats seemingly as much to remind himself as anyone else, is "No mountain is worth a life, the summit is a bonus". It did not stop him attempting to summit in 1995 though. "It's always difficult to enjoy it on top of the mountain because you know you have to get back down".

Descending is always harder, Hinkes says. "You're exhausted – particularly if you burn up loads of calories going 'yahoo!' on the summit like some people do. You have to keep yourself under control for the descent.

Death is an inescapable fact of high-altitude mountaineering.

"You find lots of bodies on the north side of Everest," he told the Alpine Club audience matter-of-factly. After all, who is going to bring them down?

"The deaths of other mountaineers do cross your mind," he says, "but I'm not going to stop climbing just because somebody dies. And when somebody does die, I'm not going to be shocked out of my box thinking 'Oh I didn't know that could happen', because I know it can, just as I know it can on a car journey."

Getting enough food is a crucial aspect of Hinkes' back-to-back climbs expedition. "Doing an 8000er is like running three marathons. You can lose stones in weight because you are burning off calories every day and can't carry enough food to get them back. You'd have trouble eating that much food anyway because it doesn't assimilate properly at altitude. The key is to have a good cook at base camp and plenty of food." This means egg and chips, bacon sandwiches and other "real" food. The mere mention of dehydrated food makes Hinkes splutter: "I wouldn't eat it if it was given to me free. It's revolting for a start and won't reconstitute properly on a big mountain because you need water that is boiling at 100° Celsius."

Hinkes celebrates his 43rd birthday on 23 April 1997, the day he intends to summit Lhotse. "You're at your peak in the Himalayas in your late 30s and early 40s," he maintains. "I was as fit as a butcher's dog 20 years ago but it would have been difficult to force myself to go slow and the way to get fit on big mountains is to keep pushing slowly."

For all his pragmatism, flippancy and northern brusqueness, Hinkes is very obviously relishing the task ahead. If he makes it – and he refuses to be drawn into rating his own chances of success – he is well aware that it will be largely down to his ability to keep mind, body and soul together in situations where the mountains have the final say. He is angry at any reference to the fact that he is "conquering" anything. "Mountaineers have never spoken about 'conquering' mountains. It is the media and non-climbers who talk in this way. You never conquer a mountain; a mountain lets you sneak to the top and sneak back down. It lets you have a good time or a bad time on it, but it never allows you to conquer it."

805 words

1 What record is Alan Hinkes hoping to beat?

   A to be the first Briton to reach the summit of Anapurna

   B to be the first Briton to climb the 14 highest mountains

   C to climb six of the world's highest mountains in a year

   D to climb the 14 highest mountains in a year

2 What does Hinkes find hardest about climbing?

   A coming down the mountain

   B failing to reach the summit

   C deciding not to take a risk

   D judging the weather conditions

3 What does he feel when he sees the bodies of dead climbers?

   A He finds it shocking.

   B He thinks they are just unlucky.

   C He accepts it as inevitable.

   D He gets very upset.

4 Why is food a problem for Hinkes when climbing?

   A He doesn't usually feel hungry.

   B He doesn't like dehydrated food.

   C He doesn't enjoy cooking it.

   D He doesn't like carrying it.

5 Why does he think he is the best age to climb mountains?

   A He is fitter than when he was younger.

   B He knows when to give up.

   C He can acclimatise more quickly.

   D He knows how to build up his strength.

6 Why does it annoy him when non-climbers talk about 'conquering mountains'?

   A Only climbers know what it really means.

   B It could bring him bad luck.

   C Mountains cannot be conquered.

   D Not many people succeed in doing it.

4 In this article you came across the verbs *burn up* and *given over*. Here are some other verbs which combine with *up* and/or *over*. Choose an appropriate form of one of the verbs to complete the sentences below.

end	up	hand
shut	over	take
blow		run

1 The officer _____ his keys to the supervisor.

2 The terrorists used a car bomb to _____ the building.

3 During the expedition we _____ going without food for several days.

4 Tom told the other children to _____ and listen to the teacher.

5 The Managing Director announced that they were being _____ by a multinational.

6 Unfortunately the dog chased the cat into the road where it was _____.

7 "Don't worry about it," he reassured me, "it will all _____ over in a couple of days."

8 When I retire I'm going to _____ golf.

Vocabulary

1 The following phrases appear in this article. Underline them and note their meanings.

an inescapable fact	mind, body and soul
cross your mind	rating chances of success
refuse to be drawn	final say
relishing the task ahead	reference to the fact

2 Use the phrases to complete the sentences below. You may need to alter them slightly.

1 Has it ever _____ that she might not want to see you?

2 In the race for the summit he _____ at a mere 50:50.

3 It is _____ that most people can't afford exotic holidays.

4 After the accident he had to concentrate on keeping his _____ together until he was rescued.

5 The judge went ahead and ordered a new enquiry _____ the report would not be available until next year.

6 The Prime Minister _____ on what he would do to help the homeless.

7 At the end of the meeting she was allowed to have her _____ but failed to convince them.

8 Despite the hardships to come the explorers were _____.

Writing

1 Read the text below which is a report about the incident described on page 65 of the Student's Book. What is the aim of the report and how does this affect its content?

> On 24th July at 7.30 p.m. I received an order to drive to junction 11 on the M5 motorway to assist my colleagues in moving a group of travellers and their vehicles. I arrived at 7.40 p.m. and joined approximately fifty police officers on the slip road. There was a five-mile tailback of cars on the northbound carriageway.
>
> The travellers and their vehicles were blocking all four lanes of the motorway including the hard shoulder. Some of the vehicles were in a poor condition and had apparently broken down.
>
> We received instructions from a senior officer to approach the convoy and encourage them to leave the motorway as quickly as possible. As we approached, some of the travellers began to throw objects at us. These appeared to be rocks and stones from the edge of the motorway. No police officers were hit but we were ordered to return to where we had parked our vehicles and collect our riot shields.
>
> At 9 p.m. we returned to the motorway ...

2 How would you describe the tone of the report? Underline the words and phrases which convey this.

3 Read the report and the article in the Student's Book again and finish the concluding paragraph. You should keep the paragraph factual but you can add details of your own.

Vocabulary

1 **Wordbuilding.** Look at these words which appear in the unit and complete the table.

NOUN	ADJECTIVE	VERB
survival	*survival*	*survive*
injury	_____	_____
_____	comparative	_____
divorce	_____	_____
_____	_____	argue
_____	_____	harm
_____	broken	_____
_____	_____	attract
_____	descriptive	_____
report	_____	_____

2 Use the correct form of the word in brackets to complete the following sentences. What part of speech is it?

1 Fortunately, as a soldier, he had been taught _____ (survival) tactics during his training.

2 The _____ (injury) passengers were rescued within minutes.

3 It is unfair to _____ (comparative) an amateur sportsman with a professional.

4 There is no evidence that children of _____ (divorce) parents are more likely to turn into criminals.

5 _____ (argue) the best lifestyle is the one you feel most comfortable with.

6 Cigarettes and alcohol are known to be _____ (harm) in excess.

7 Eleanor will _____ (broken) her father's heart when she gives up her swimming career.

8 The life of a mountaineer has no _____ (attract) for me.

9 The article gave a detailed _____ (describe) of the place where the travellers had camped.

10 Have you _____ (report) your missing bike to the police?

3 Prefixes and suffixes. Group the following into prefixes and suffixes

un less in ful im dis extra inter

Now use the prefixes and suffixes to make new words out of those in the box.

> happy possible ordinary palatable action
> fit home regard used to decided
> fortunate agreement certainty professional
> employed help satisfied

Can you think of at least one more example for each of the suffixes and prefixes? Check them in your dictionary.

4 Complete the sentences 1–8 using a word with a suitable prefix or suffix from the box in 3. Use each prefix and suffix once only.

1 Edward was totally _____ with his exam results.

2 There is a high degree of _____ surrounding which players will be selected for the team.

3 A large grant from the fund will go towards setting up shelters for the _____.

4 The officer was criticized for his _____ during the riot when he was seen sitting in his car during the height of the confrontation.

5 It would be _____ if those who were to be made redundant could be told as soon as possible.

6 It is quite _____ to force such large numbers of people to disperse quietly.

7 The _____ scenes of violence outside the stadium have surprised and shocked us all.

8 It is vital that _____ of any kind between the witnesses is prevented before and during the trial.

English in Use

Part 4

1 Quickly read through the text. Decide what part of speech you will need in each gap.

2 Insert the correct form of the word given in capitals below into each of the gaps.

> Many people remain in (0) __unhappy__ relationships where conflict and
> (1)_____ are the norm.
>
> They do not realise how (2)_____ this can be, nor do they believe that it is
> (3)_____ to talk about their problems. Some believe that
> (4)_____ is good enough and it is too much to expect to have a truly
> (5)_____ relationship.
> (6)_____ many marriages end in divorce because couples have not realized how
> (7)_____ it can be to ignore their difficulties. The mere thought of consulting a stranger is (8) _____ to them.

0 HAPPY
1 ARGUE
2 DAMAGE
3 CONSTRUCT
4 SURVIVE
5 SATISFY
6 FORTUNATE
7 HARM
8 PALATABLE

3 **Register.** Make complete sentences using the following phrases from Unit 5. Which sentences sound more informal or formal? In what sort of text might you find your sentences?

I'm feeling a bit

The Minister announced

There's no point in

Talks have broken down

It should be avoided

It was absolute chaos

Structure

1 Punctuation. Read this text carefully. Some necessary punctuation marks (speech marks and apostrophes) have been omitted. Punctuate the text correctly.

PSYCHOLOGIST JOHN GOTTMAN believes parents should teach their children to deal with feelings.

Try to see things from a childs view. When a birthday present arrived for his brother and Kyle said it wasnt fair, his dad said: When its your birthday Grandma will probably send you a package. Gottman explains: While this statement explains the logic of the situation, it denies Kyles feelings at that moment. On top of feeling jealous, Kyle feels angry that his dad doesnt understand his position. Imagine if his dad were to respond: You wish Grandma had sent you a package, too – I bet that makes you feel jealous. Realizing his father understands the way he feels makes Kyle more receptive.

Parents often set limits on inappropriate behaviour such as rudeness. But as Gottman says: Its not easy for children to change the way they feel about a situation. A childs sadness, fear or rage doesnt just disappear because a parent says: Stop crying. If we tell a child how she ought to feel, it just makes her distrust what she does feel, leading to a loss of self-esteem. But if we tell her she has the right to her feelings, but there may be a better way to express them, her self-esteem is left intact. Also she knows she has an adult on her side.

---

2 Direct and reported speech. Turn the following sentences into reported or direct speech as appropriate.

1 "What we are trying to do is to keep an eye on these convoys and prevent them from camping on common land."

2 His research also suggests that anger between spouses is not harmful except when accompanied by more lethal emotions like contempt or disgust.

3 News Reader: Have there been any complaints?
   Kate Simpson: I believe so, yes.

4 Councillor Johnson confirmed today that Equip would be the new owners of the sports hall.

5 "Don't mention this matter to anyone, Frank. It's extremely delicate!"

6 The regional manager claimed that there was a significant lack of social amenities such as sports facilities.

7 "This office equipment badly needs to be modernized. Look at this typewriter – it's completely out of date!"

8 He says if he's not going to be selected, he'd rather know now.

3 Constructions after reporting verbs. The reporting verbs on the left appear in the texts in this Workbook. Match the verbs with one or more of the constructions on the right.

1	maintained	a	to do something
2	refused	b	someone to somebody
3	repeated	c	to something
4	told	d	something from somebody
5	introduced		
6	said	e	that something was the case
7	explained		
8	responded	f	somebody about something

Now use a suitable reporting verb from the list above in these sentences.

1 Hinkes _____ that people are fittest in their 30s and 40s.

2 The climber _____ to tell us whether he would be successful or not.

3 He _____ his view that it wasn't worth taking unnecessary risks.

4 They were _____ that many bodies are found on the north side of Everest.

5 The club's president _____ the speaker as a world famous mountaineer.

6 The psychologist _____ that it was important to see things from a child's point of view.

7 Gottman _____ that it wasn't easy for children to change the way they felt about a situation.

8 Kyle _____ positively to his father's suggestion that he was feeling jealous.

6 Culture Vultures

English in Use

Part 1

1 Read the following article about an unsuccessful musical, ignoring the spaces for the moment. What explanation is given for its failure?

Broadway's biggest musical flop

The legendary American singer-songwriter Paul Simon has (0)____ another record to his collection, but unlike his many previous (1)____, this time the 'achievement' is for (2)____ the most expensive flop musical ever on Broadway. 'The Capeman' features the true story of a cape-wearing Puerto Rican immigrant who (3)____ two teenagers to death in 1959. It opened in New York just five weeks ago, but is already on the (4)____ of closing, with an estimated loss of $11 million, much of it Simon's own money. One of the most (5)____ songwriters of his generation, Simon was abroad when the decision to pull the (6)____ on his first musical was (7)____ to a tearful cast yesterday. He is reported by friends to be (8)____ upset and says he will never do another Broadway show.

Simon and his backers had hoped that the show's big advance sales would (9)____ its chances of success, but many of these sales were only options, which were not (10)____ up after the show was panned by the critics. Yet at the outset, 'The Capeman' seemed to have a winning (11)____, for in addition to Simon's pivotal role, it had words by Nobel laureate Derek Walcott and choreography by Mark Morris. However, the show was unconvincing and didn't hang together. Part of the (12)____ for this may be the fact that it went through three directors. The latest, Jerry Zaks, (13)____ the opening night by three weeks in the hope that things would gel, but even after this, he couldn't pull it (14)____. Despite their admiration for Simon's music, critics (15)____ that 'The Capeman' never came alive dramatically and was much too long. As one reviewer said, "It was like watching a mortally wounded animal."

⏱ **300 words**

2 Now underline the best alternative from A, B, C or D to fit spaces 1–15. An example (0) is given.

	A	B	C	D
0	added	B included	C joined	D increased
1	rewards	B verdicts	C awards	D gifts
2	forging	B crafting	C founding	D creating
3	killed	B murdered	C injured	D stabbed
4	margin	B limit	C verge	D brim
5	cheered	B acclaimed	C welcomed	D approved
6	cork	B lid	C plug	D top
7	asserted	B argued	C advised	D announced
8	extremely	B absolutely	C widely	D completely
9	develop	B grow	C inspire	D boost
10	taken	B made	C brought	D put
11	procedure	B formula	C method	D way
12	answer	B indication	C reason	D intention
13	suppressed	B delayed	C interrupted	D transferred
14	down	B on	C up	D off
15	demanded	B accused	C insisted	D urged

Reading

1 To the right are four reviews of art exhibitions. First, look through the questions. Then scan the reviews to find the answers. Sometimes, more than one answer is possible.

A Show 48

B ABSOLUT NeW

C Propositions

D Technosophia 1

Which exhibition or exhibitions:

has language as a theme?	1 ____
features local artists?	2 ____
includes music?	3 ____
is housed at the top of a building?	4 ____
shows a film?	5 ____
has received commercial funding?	6 ____
involves spectators as part of the work?	7 ____
is part of an on-going event?	8 ____ 9 ____
is compared favourably to other exhibitions?	10 ____
is seen as a mix of old and new?	11 ____
includes work which reproduces that of another artist?	12 ____
has a piece done jointly by two artists?	13 ____
has a work using household objects?	14 ____
is exhibiting someone who has featured in TV programmes?	15 ____

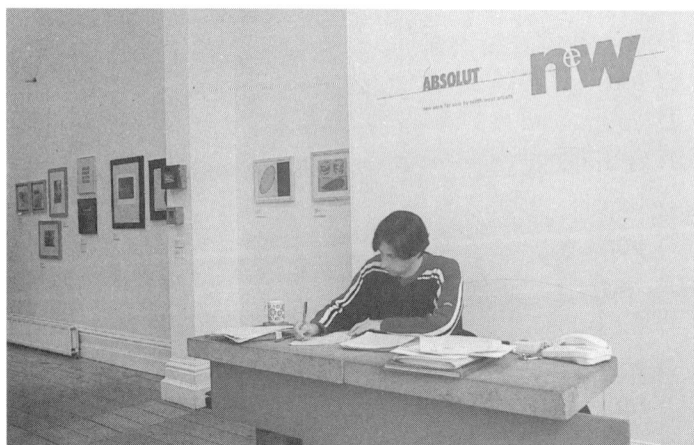

Show 48

CITY RACING, LONDON

To use a football cliché, this is a show of three halves. First there is *Brian Dawn Chalkley presents Motherload*, a neon-lit collection of wall-mounted objects and video projections by 11 artists. This includes David Harrison's *Alice Springs*, a Picasso-esque recycling of a deep-fat fryer, some bed springs, a pair of floral brooches and a twist of pink rubber, all skilfully transformed into the Alice of the title. Highlights of the video programme are Edwin David's tragic piece on Nico, called *All Tomorrow's Parties,* and Chalkley's own nocturnal road movie. Secondly, there is Jemima Stehli's installation: three, life-sized photographs where Stehli acts out Allen Jones's controversial furniture-sculptures. Stehli adopts the poses for Jones's original *Table 1, Table 2* and *Chair*, but it is unclear whether we are supposed to view this as critique or homage. Finally, Hilary Lloyd's *Sal* is a video installation presented as a room-sized tableau, where we are left to consider Sal as she mooches and fidgets, while off-screen we hear distant voices and passing cars. Why we have been asked to consider this mundane scenario is unclear until a brown dog jumps up to attract Sal's attention; from this point on we realize that, as viewers, we have been doing much the same as Sal – watching and waiting. Lloyd cleverly establishes the presence of the audience within the work itself, reflecting us back onto ourselves.

Matthew Higgs

235 words

ABSOLUT NeW

CASTLEFIELD GALLERY, MANCHESTER

If, in music, Manchester-cool has come to mean slouch walks and morose attitude, the city's art image has for decades been a rather purist one. The artist-run Castlefield Gallery is flourishing creatively, if struggling financially. This sponsored show has works by over 30 artists currently living in the region and many are moderately priced. The range of work on display indicates that the Manchester scene has begun a process of self-liberation from the painterly seriousness of its past. While Liam Spencer's gloomy, urban landscapes or Ben Cook's lemon abstracts might be seen to be keeping to the traditional Manchester style, some cultural irreverence has crept in elsewhere. This is mostly achieved by those willing to own up to the fact that the lens of the photographic, movie and video camera has radically altered and conditioned our visual experiences and artistic responses. So, for example, Anneke Pettican and Kerri Moogan present collaborative stills with the enchanting blur of city lights seen from a late night ride home; Nick Crowe's blue-black motorbike R-type transparency print is a Kieferesque icon of escape from the dead end of the century. These works have Manchester cool a-plenty but, well, they're more connected.

Robert Clark

205 words

Propositions

CAIRN GALLERY, NAILSWORTH

Quietly occupying some attic rooms in the small town of Nailsworth, this is an truly magical contemporary art gallery, run by poet Tom Clark. 'Propositions' is a continuing series of exhibitions that began last summer. For each show, three artists are invited to present work, together with a statement or proposition. This particular exhibition, though, is slightly different: instead of individual artists, there is work from three separate publishing groups. Installed in the first room is the extensive *Audio Arts* archive. Established in 1973 by artist William Furlong, *Audio Arts* is a quarterly magazine on cassette, offering recordings of conversations with, and talks by, artists. There are of course listening facilities here. In fact, the room feels like some nostalgic recording studio. In the adjoining room, *Morning Star* books, based in Edinburgh, have a small green book on display, simply entitled *Irish*. Inside is the seven-line poem 'Irisch' by Paul Celan, together with five very different English translations of it, and one in Gaelic. Accompanying the book are seven gouache paintings by Sol LeWitt. The third room exhibits four prints from *Peninsula*, an artists' cooperative based in Holland. Richard Long's print is stunning. Long's work can seem out of place in the grand museums, lavish coffee table books, and documentaries where it frequently appears, but here, within the intimacy of the Cairn Gallery, its beauty and integrity shine.

Julian Warren

230 words

Technosophia I: overpromised

THE SWISS INSTITUTE, NEW YORK

Strangers to New York City might be surprised to learn about a hip art opening on Broadway, but then, times are changing. These days, most galleries are filled with rather uncontroversial stuff, though some artists are trying to break this stalemate. Artists like those at the Swiss Institute, who are attempting to give expression to the sounds and sights of a young generation. Initiated by Swiss artists Eric Schumacher and Andrea Clavadetscher, 'Technosophia I' is the first in a series of three installations. Everything about the exhibition reflects a less rigid approach, creating a real live action experience. In the 'sound lounge', crafted by Bessie Nager and Ali Janka, a huge silver tubular padded network hangs cloud-like from the ceiling. Hidden inside it, speakers play a techno jukebox selection by 22 different artists and DJs. Central to the group's work is a desire to associate art with the everyday – here, club culture and its offshoots. Colour photocopies of the DJs and artists are stuck loosely to a white wall, echoing the anti-art tactics of the Fluxus and Dada movements. It seems ironic that it is European rather than US artists who are breaking the mould in New York, but perhaps it's because they're not interested in producing work that conforms to market demands. 'Technosophia I' (an intentional hybrid of techno and philosophy) is a burst of clean, honest fun.

Jane Czyzselska

230 words

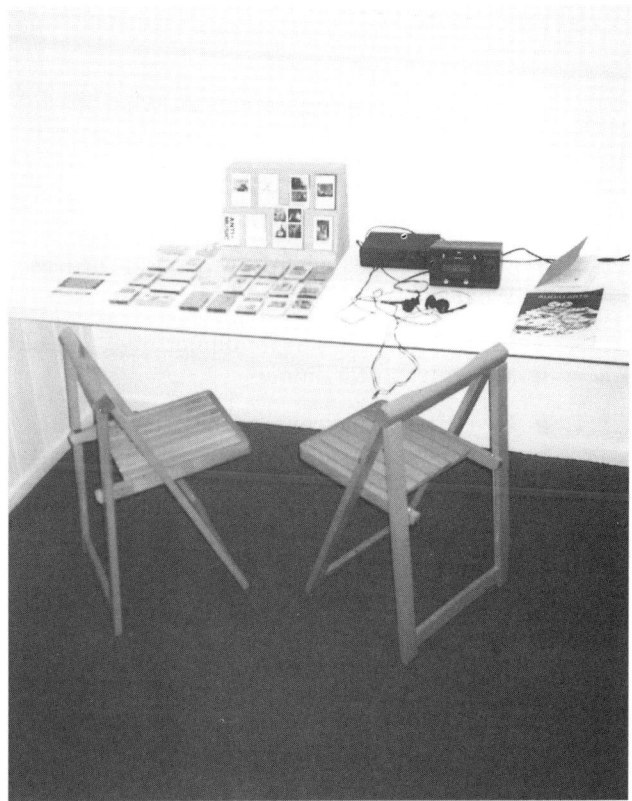

2 Find the following words in the reviews and match them to meanings 1–12. The reviews are given in brackets.

a	homage (A)	1	conventional
b	mooches (A)	2	mixture of two things
c	morose (B)	3	principle
d	irreverence (B)	4	related things
e	enchanting (B)	5	stands around
f	nostalgic (C)	6	behaves as expected
g	lavish (C)	7	charming
h	integrity (C)	8	respect or admiration
i	uncontroversial (D)	9	luxurious
j	offshoots (D)	10	sentimental
k	conforms (D)	11	miserable
l	hybrid (D)	12	disrespect

Structure

1 Read the following pairs of sentences. What are the possible differences in meaning or implication?

1 a I think Frank's going to fall in the water.
  b I think Frank will fall in the water.

2 a What are you going to do when John arrives?
  b What will you do when John arrives?

3 a Are you going to stay for dinner?
  b Will you stay for dinner?

4 a He isn't going to come to the party.
  b He won't come to the party.

5 a I'm going to write to him about the problem.
  b I'll write to him about the problem.

2 Complete these sentences using either the simple future or the future continuous and the verbs in brackets.

a On 26th October 2028 a large asteroid _____ (pass) close to our earth.

b Astronomers _____ (prepare) for the event for quite a few months beforehand.

c Some calculations show that it _____ (come) within 30,000 miles of earth.

d However, most scientists say it _____ (not, be) closer than 600,000 miles.

e Either way, people all over the world _____ (keep) a careful eye on the news throughout 2028!

3 Finish these predictions about the future in your own words.

a Within the next five years, the Internet _____
_____
_____

b Traffic congestion is going to become so severe that _____
_____
_____

c In 20 years' time, we won't be using books. Instead, _____
_____
_____

English in Use

Part 4

1 Read this short article about the film *Romeo + Juliet*. Then look at gaps 1–8 and make suitable words from the ones given in capital letters. An example is given.

If you're one of those (0)____*purists*____ who believes Shakespeare on film is too (1)_____ for words, you'll probably find Baz Luhrmann's *Romeo + Juliet* doubly (2)_____ . Though faithful to the plot, the story has been (3)_____ to modern-day Verona Beach; automatic weapons take the place of swords and daggers; and Shakespeare's text is sometimes made (4)_____ by a booming soundtrack. However, in all (5)_____, I believe this is one of the most brilliant Shakespeare films ever made. Indeed, I suggest that not since the 17th century has a (6)_____ of 'Romeo and Juliet' been quite so in tune with its audience's (7)_____. Still, this masterpiece is bound to be loathed by (8)_____. It's super cool, it's too sexy, and it comes too close to proving that if Shakespeare were around today, he'd be making Hollywood blockbusters!

0 PURE
1 OUTRAGE
2 OBJECT
3 LOCATE
4 COMPREHEND

5 SERIOUS
6 PRODUCE
7 SENSIBLE
8 TRADITION

Writing

1 Read this review of the computer game *Riven* and identify what is dealt with in each paragraph, ignoring the errors for the moment.

Riven, for anyone who has been on another planet recently, is the newly-published sequel to the most succesful computer game of all time, *Myst*. Produced by Broderbund, both are fantacy adventure games, where the player visits different virtuel worlds, attempting to solve an extremly intricate mystery.

With the arrival of this wonderfull sequel, even the biggest fans of *Myst* will find it hard to go back, for *Riven* is, quite simply, the perfect aventure game. The graphics are even better than before, with a constant attention to detail in the special affects. The landscapes are ecsquisite, the buildings and transport craft highly imagineative. There is also an opportunity to explor the sea, where you pass through a beautiful underwater world of blues and greens.

As for the game itself, it is if anything slightly simpler than before, particlarly in the introductery stages. It is based on that previous wining formula of visual observation, lateral thinking and 'try it and see'. This last quality is especialy clever, for it allows the player to experiment freely, without worrying about the consequenses.

There are no negativ points to this game, though anyone hoping to buy it should first assess the amount of avaliable memory on their computer – and check this against the small print on the packaging before purchase. Graphics sometimes have their prize, as computers can run slow when overloaded.

Riven is compelling, and immensley satisfying when it reveels its secrets. It is highly reccomended for people of any age, who will find that it quite literally takes them into another world.

🕛 **260 words**

2 Now proof-read the review, correcting the 20 spelling errors.

Welcome to the Real World

Reading

1 Read the main text of this article, ignoring the missing paragraphs. Note the period of time described.

Putting classroom before catwalk

Britain's newest supermodel is resisting the bright lights of New York's catwalks to study for her A levels, despite landing a six-figure cosmetics contract. Sarah Thomas, aged 16, caught the fashion world's attention in October, where she collected £6,500 a day in her half-term break.

(1) __C__ ✓

This six-figure deal is a coveted step on the route to full supermodel status: other top models who have performed the role in the past include Helena Christensen and Rachel Hunter.

(2) __E__ ✓

very quickly

Two days after taking the last one, she was whisked off to Paris for a month to work for the Ford model agency. To begin with, she almost wished she hadn't come. "I met so many girls who'd been out there for a month and hadn't worked. I thought 'This isn't for me'."

(3) __A__ ✓

Now following A-level courses in maths, physics and design technology, she insists on staying to complete these and take the exams. The cosmetics contract will involve 15 days' work, mostly in the US. Some of it can be fitted into school holidays, but there is an inevitable clash of interests.

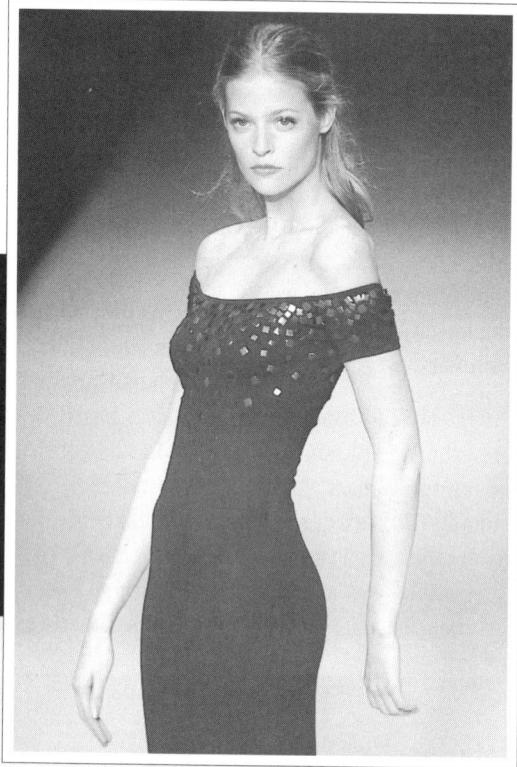

(4) __B__ G

Does she regret having had to do this? It seems not. "I want to get good qualifications; I enjoy school and being with my friends, just being normal. If I modelled full-time, every day I'd be with people I don't know. I know I'm nearly 17, but it just isn't for me at the moment."

(5) __B__ G

What do her parents feel about these choices? Her father, Peter Thomas, who runs a garage near Norwich, was initially keen for his daughter to leave school and start modelling full-time. Both parents have been very supportive of Sarah's modelling opportunities, and usually one or other of them has accompanied her on trips abroad.

(6) __D__ ✓

Maybe not, although it clearly does have its attractions – Sarah's next trip will take her to Miami, then back to New York. "I do like New York," she said. "There are so many shops." Thank goodness, the girl is human!

2 Now look at missing paragraphs A–G and fit them in the gaps. There is one extra that you do not need.

A
However, after a few days, she was selected to do the Chanel catwalk show, and was on her way. At the same time, she knew that school was an unfinished chapter in her life, to which she wanted to return.

B
Sarah quite definitely plans some sort of career in modelling, though. "If I model full-time for a couple of years I can earn enough money to go to university. I'm not sure what I want to study yet. I'm interested in design, but not fashion – architectural design, perhaps, and technical drawing."

C
After seeing her in action, talent scouts from the American cosmetics company Cover Girl invited her for an interview. She did a screen test in London and got the job.

D
It was this brief exposure to the fashion business that caused an about-turn in Sarah's father. "I've seen what the life is like: there's a lot of drugs. They've got a lot of time off and a lot of money. It's not the life for someone of 16."

E
Sarah was discovered at 14 by model agent Sarah Reynolds, who spotted her at a local cricket match. Ms Reynolds signed her up straight away, but for these first two years, Sarah couldn't devote much time to her new career, as she was too busy studying for 9 GCSE exams.

F
Not all the work involves foreign travel, though. One recent task was to model local football team Norwich City's new strip, designed by Bruce Oldfield.

G
In fact, her head has given Sarah the necessary time off to fulfil her engagements, without hesitation. Sarah is known to be the strictest disciplinarian when it comes to catching up with assignments. "It's a bit difficult," she said. "I've just been given a load of design technology coursework, and the phone hasn't stopped ringing all day. I've already had to turn down some offers because of the exams."

In 1998, Sarah Thomas announced her decision to quit the catwalk, saying she could not tolerate the fashion industry's obsession with skinniness.

3 Complete these definitions, using words and phrases from the article.

a If something _catches the attention_ of the public, they notice it.

b Something that is _coveted_ is highly desirable.

c When a person is _sign up_, it means that they have accepted a contract.

d A _clash of interests_ usually involves you in having to turn something down.

e A _talent scouts_ has to look out for people likely to succeed.

f If someone has an _about-turn_, they completely change their mind about something.

g A _disciplinarian_ has very precise rules of behaviour.

Structure

1 Complete the following sentences with *wish*, *regret* or *miss*. Then say whether these statements are true or false, based on your understanding of the article on page 32.

a Sarah Thomas doesn't _____ that she accepted the Cover Girl contract.

b When she was studying for her GCSEs, Sarah _____ she could have spent more time on the catwalks.

c Once Chanel had offered her work, Sarah no longer _____ being in Paris.

d However, at that time, she also _____ her life at school.

e The school head _____ Sarah didn't have to interrupt her studies to go to America.

f Sarah doesn't want to model full-time yet, as she would _____ her friends.

2 Complete these sentences using a suitable auxiliary or modal.

a I wish you _____ tie your shoelaces; I'm sure you'll trip over them, otherwise.

b We regret _____ to announce these redundancies, but there is no other way of saving the company.

c Don't you wish you _____ just take off on holiday for a week and leave the in-tray behind?

d Working mothers often wish they _____ have to juggle so many responsibilities.

e Paul really regrets not _____ learned Spanish at school; it would be so useful in his job.

f Judith really wishes her husband _____ work such long hours; she's worried he'll burn out.

g I wish the council _____ clear up all this litter in the street; it's getting to be a health hazard.

h The office party was a big disappointment and John regretted _____ there, with no one interesting to talk to.

3 Imagine you had to leave your home for a whole year. What would you miss doing? Write five sentences like the example below.

I would miss sitting in the garden in the spring.

_____

_____

_____

_____

_____

4 Finish the sentences, using the information given. The first one is done as an example.

a I forgot to get the car serviced and it has broken down.

If only I had *remembered to get the car serviced! Then it wouldn't have broken down.*

b Sally applied too late for the job. She heard later that she would probably have been offered it.

If only Sally hadn't _____

_____

c Just before taking his school exams, Nigel spent a lot of time clubbing; he didn't do very well.

If only Nigel had spent _____

_____

d Greta's parents quashed her idea of taking a year out between school and university, so she went straight there. She hated it and left after two months.

If only Greta's parents had allowed her _____

_____

_____

e I want to help you with your homework, so that you could get a better mark.

If only you would _____

_____

English in Use

Part 2

Read the text about Damon Rose and fill in the spaces, writing one word only. An example is given.

'So, I'm blind. Why shouldn't I be a BBC television director?'

BBC Television has accepted its first blind man on to (0)___its___ trainee directors' course. 27-year-old Damon Rose beat 350 applicants to join the BBC last December and (1)_____ first report, about cars and the visually impaired, (2)_____ be broadcast on Tuesday. Mr Rose said that he found (3)_____ totally unsurprising that someone (4)_____ could not see should want to work (5)_____ television, particularly as more blind people 'watch' TV (6)_____ listen to the radio. "It's not (7)_____ a visual medium – there is sound."

He was a television addict (8)_____ he lost his sight at the age of 13 and says that the many hours spent watching have given him an in-depth knowledge, (9)_____ has already proved very useful. He argues that (10)_____ the job of a television director is analysed, the vast majority of the work is carried out in the office. "Directors don't do the camera work, (11)_____ is the whole point. They direct. I plan everything in my head and rely (12)_____ members of the crew to tell me what is in shot."

Ian Macrae, editor of the BBC's disability programmes unit, said Mr Rose's training, including research, television writing and a camera-work course, was what (13)_____ trainee would do. Explaining the recruitment policy, Mr Macrae said: "There aren't (14)_____ disabled people on television, and one reason for this is that there are all (15)_____ few disabled people in the industry. We aim to address both these things."

⏱ **265 words**

Vocabulary

Complete this puzzle using words from this unit. There are clues opposite. What word is revealed?

1   _ _ _ _ _ _ **M**
2   **S** _ _ _ _ _ _ _
3   _ _ **T** _ _ _ _
4   **M** _ _ _ _ _
5   _ _ _ _ _ _ _ _ **Y**
6   **B** _ _ _ _ _
7   **S** _ _ _ _ _ _
8 **P** _ _ _ _ _ _ _ _

1 Mariah Carey and Madonna both achieved this before they were 20.
2 For many people, this is the most important factor in a job.
3 Everybody encounters these in life at some point!
4 Washing-up is often described as this.
5 If you lose your job, you may be offered this.
6 Stressed executives often hit this at a relatively young age.
7 A good adjective to describe a lighthouse-keeper's job.
8 Talent or skill.

English in Use

Part 5

Read the following job advertisement. Then, using the information given,
complete the informal letter to Jenny, using no more than two words in
each gap. Do not use any words which appear in the advertisement.

Administrator, Southfield Arts Festival

This post provides assistance to the Director in the planning and
preparation of our prestigious annual festival. The administrator's
busy schedule will extend beyond the normal working day and
at weekends. Consequently, the successful applicant will be
dedicated and hard-working, able to work under pressure, and
have proven organizational skills.

Duties will include the selection and booking of venues; the
compilation of a new mailing list; the preparation and
distribution of publicity material.

Generous terms are offered to the right person, including a
substantial monthly salary and a relocation package.

Applications to…

Informal letter

Dear Jenny

I've just seen an ad for administrator of the Southfield Arts
Festival — it would suit you down to the ground! It looks as though
the administrator's role is really to give the Director
(0)___back-up___ in getting things ready for the Festival, which
is a very (1)_____ event, you know. It happens every year
here in Southfield. The ad does say the job has long and
(2)_____ hours — including Saturdays and Sundays!
But then I know how you relish a heavy (3)_____ !
    You need to be able to show you can (4)_____
stress, as well as giving them (5)_____ how well
you can manage things — that should be dead easy for you, with
your track record!
    The job includes (6)_____ suitable places to hold
concerts and firming up the arrangements,
(7)_____ names and addresses, and creating
leaflets (and then (8)_____ in envelopes!)
    If you got the job, you wouldn't be (9)_____
for peanuts, either — they would even pay for you to
(10)_____ down here!
    What are you waiting for — get that c.v. off today.

love
Ruth

Writing

1 In Part 1 of the Writing paper, you should try to expand on the points given where possible. Read all the information in the task below and then decide how sentences a–h could be added to, using the information given and your own ideas. Make improvements where you can; for example, try to avoid the sentences starting with 'I' all the time. Remember not to lift from the question, apart from key words.

> The following article about a work exchange programme appeared in your college magazine recently. You participated in the same programme, but your experience was totally different from the writer's.
>
> Read the notes you made and then write a letter to the editor of the magazine, putting your side of the story. You should use your own words as far as possible.

WORK EXCHANGE UTTER SHAMBLES *unfair!*

At the start of the summer term, I signed up for the work exchange programme run by this college. I heard nothing <u>for weeks</u>, but on the last day of term I was told by e-mail that I had been placed with a company in London and was to report there the following Monday.

I did... phone + letter, 10 days later

Nothing else! There was absolutely <u>no help</u> with travel arrangements or accommodation, <u>no useful advice about what to take</u> and no info about what I would be doing!

come on – you're not a kid!

Fortunately, my parents stepped in and booked me a flight, as well as finding me somewhere to live through a friend of theirs. So, off I went – rather nervously – and on the Monday morning I set off to find the company. They were based a long way from the centre (so much for what we were led to believe) and when I turned up at reception, they didn't have a clue who I was! It took three phone calls to get everything sorted out – and for that week, I wasn't given anything <u>remotely interesting</u> to do.

college only said London

perhaps this says more about you?

how?

Although things <u>improved</u>, I really wouldn't recommend anyone spending their summer like I did. It was an utter shambles.   *Carl Lama*

my placement was opposite: v. useful work experience, friendly colleagues...

a The title of your article is biased.

b I enrolled in the programme.

c I heard about my placement within ten days, by phone and in writing.

d There was no undertaking from the college to arrange accommodation.

e I find the writer's complaint about the lack of advice unnecessary – I mean, we aren't kids.

f I don't recall the college guaranteeing a company in <u>central</u> London.

g The writer says the work wasn't "remotely interesting" to begin with – he has a problem.

h I find it strange that the writer doesn't mention the rest of his stay.

2 Now write the complete letter, including these sentences, suitably linked. Your conclusion should address the final notes in the question.

Going Places

Reading

1 As you read each numbered paragraph 1–11 decide what it is about. Think of a phrase or sentence which summarizes it for you.

The Natural Traveller

Guy Marks tests out homeopathic remedies for the ailing traveller.

1

I like drugs; good honest conventional pharmaceutical medicines. So when it was suggested that I give homeopathic remedies a try, I was more than a little sceptical. I was surprised to find that there are homoeopathic kits aimed specifically at the traveller, so the least I could do as a traveller was to give them a go. A couple of weeks' holiday didn't work out as a significant trial – I'm sorry, but I just didn't get ill. When I joined a group of 25 people travelling on an overland truck, however, it was a different matter. Some were staying with the trip for six months and there would always be people with ailments. The kit consisted of 36 remedies for the traveller – all packed up in a neat little green case.

2

My first impression was that a lot of thought had been put into the design. The box is made of strong plastic which makes it easily packable and portable. The vials containing the little pills have screw caps which is a lot more practical for travelling than the cork stoppers that are used by some other homeopathic pharmacies.

3

Two sheets of information are provided. The first is a general introduction to the subject explaining the bare minimum of the principles of homeopathy. The second information sheet lists common complaints and suggests a number of remedies that might be suitable for treating the symptoms.

4

The first treatment I gave was when a girl got hit in the face by a swinging door caught in the wind. It was quite a serious accident and Alberto, a doctor on board, put a couple of cross stitch plasters over the gash that opened up above her eye. After a deal of commotion and sympathy, the mood settled and I gave her an Arnica from the kit. Amazingly, there was very little swelling and her face never even bruised – spooky. Alberto was unimpressed.

5

On another occasion someone's hand swelled up like a cow's udder as a result of a mosquito bite. Apis from the kit brought the swelling under control in about twenty minutes. On the other hand, the swelling on someone's legs caused by a kind of heat rash didn't respond to Apis, Belladonna, Ledum or anything else I could find. Cantharis, however, did bring some relief to a case of sunburn. These were all cases of swellings where the cause was pretty plain to establish, but the treatments, even with the information available, were a bit hit and miss.

6

Altitude sickness high in the Peruvian Andes is something that should have been relatively easy to treat. The locals chew copious quantities of Coca leaves to combat the effects of the thin air, so the little vial of Coca tablets were easy to diagnose. Unfortunately they didn't work and I'm not quite sure why the minimal near-non-existent dose principle of homeopathic remedies should work when local knowledge has found that the more of the stuff you chew the better.

7

There were a couple of rather unexpected problems that I actually did manage to find treatments for. The first was that rather comical disorder – piles. Reading between the lines of the [1]*materia medica* I figured that the phrases "refreshes the parts Arnica cannot reach" and "reduces after-effect of lengthy sitting" meant that Bellis Perennis was the remedy to use for the offending haemorrhoids. Sure enough it worked.

8

The biggest surprise, though, was one girl who joined the trip not feeling at her best. After a few weeks she realized she was pregnant and morning sickness took its toll. Well, there wasn't a traveller's remedy for this, but the closest ailment I could find was travel sickness, for which Cocculus was suggested. Believe it or not, the remedy relieved her symptoms.

9

The kit continued its journey for a full six months and it has to be said that some things worked and others didn't. It seems to me that this is an entire area of medicine that warrants careful consideration. As a person with no experience in this field and a sceptical outlook, I was still able to find remedies that were of genuine benefit. My scepticism has been tempered, and my knowledge broadened. I like to think I have an open mind about homeopathy, even if some medical doctors do not.

10

As I understand it, the classical concept of homeopathy is to treat a person rather than a symptom – to take a holistic approach. Because most of us aren't accustomed to doing this, there is a temptation to use a kit like this in the wrong way. It seemed quite natural to look up the ailment and expect to find a remedy prescribed for its cure.

11

Had I set out with a box full of conventional drugs and no medical training, my results would probably also have been hit and miss. The great difference is that the homeopathic remedies are non-toxic so there is nothing to be lost by prescribing the wrong remedy. Conventional medicine, however, is dangerous in the hands of the unqualified.

[1] Materia medica: Science of drugs

🕐 **870 words**

---

2 Choose suitable headings for the first five numbered sections. There are more headings than sections.

  A Helpful Hints
  B More not Less
  C A Bit of a Disaster
  D Travel Trial
  E Packaged and Portable
  F Cure All
  G Conventional Attitudes
  H Some Successes

3 Now look at paragraphs 6–11. Match the statements with the paragraphs. You will find that some choices are needed more than once.

  There's no harm in trying.   1 _11_

  The aim is to treat the whole person. 2 _10_

  There were some surprising successes. 3 _7_   4 _8_

  Sometimes more is better.   5 _6_

  It could be hit and miss.   6 _11_   7 _9_

4 Find these phrases (a–d) in the article and match them to the best meaning below. Then find phrases in the article for the two extra meanings.

  a hit and miss 2
  b more than a little 3
  c bring some relief 4
  d combat the effects 6

  1 not prejudiced To have an open-mind
  2 might work or not nothing to be lost
  3 very
  4 make it a bit better
  5 no danger in
  6 reduce the influence of

5 **Style.** Look at the openings of each of paragraphs 2–11. Decide what cohesive devices are being used from the list below:

  a linking with the previous paragraph 2,10,11
  b adding context and colour 4,5,6,7,8
  c focusing on a specific topic 2,3
  d making a general statement 9,10,11

1 - G   2 - E   3 - A   4 - C   5 - H   6 -

Vocabulary

1 The following phrases a–l occur in the article, 'The Natural Traveller'. Find them in the text and match them to the meanings 1–12 listed on the right.

a   more than a little   2

b   give them a go   10

c   it was a different matter   8

d   the bare minimum   1

e   brought under control   11

f   bring some relief   9

g   a bit hit and miss   12

h   took its toll   3

i   have an open mind   5

j   warrants careful consideration   6

k   nothing to be lost   7

l   has been tempered   4

1   as little detail as possible

2   quite a lot

3   caused some distress

4   has been reduced

5   be willing to consider new ideas

6   deserves serious attention

7   no danger in

8   the situation was not the same

9   lessened the pain

10   try them out

11   stopped from getting worse

12   liable to error

2 Fill in the gaps in these sentences by choosing from the phrases on the left in exercise 1. You may have to change the phrases slightly to fit the sentences.

1   Selecting an appropriate remedy for a particular ailment can be _____ _____.

2   I _____ when it comes to deciding where to go on holiday

3   The long journey had _____ and she looked completely exhausted.

4   The boat was going to sink anyway so there was _____ in trying to swim for the shore immediately.

5   None of us had ever been in a hot air balloon before but we decided to _____.

6   At last we found some shade under a large tree and this _____ from the burning sun.

7   Although we all knew how to swim, the thought of jumping into the cold, dark lake _____.

8   When travelling to a warmer climate I only take _____ and buy anything I need when I'm out there.

9   As the bus eventually pulled in to the loading bay we were _____ relieved to see that the children were safe and unhurt.

10   The fire brigade was called and after several hours the blaze was _____.

11   His recent experiences with alternative therapies _____ his belief that only western medicine is worthwhile.

12   Any attempt to try and cure or alleviate the disease _____.

Writing

Use your Vocabulary Resource, especially 6.2, 8.1 and 12.1.

You have been asked to give information in the form of an article about a holiday in China. The article is for a newspaper. You have been given the schedule and your task is to tell readers what they will see and do and how they will travel during the 15 days. The aim is to inform but also to recommend the trip.

Visiting the heart of China

The journey begins with an Air China non-stop flight to Beijing followed by three nights at the 4-star Xiyuan hotel in the centre of the city. During our time there you can choose between visiting the Forbidden City and the Summer Palace or take a trip out of Beijing and see the unforgettable Great Wall and the valley of the Ming tombs.

Then you fly to Wuhan …

1 Read the first paragraph of the article. What is the purpose of the phrases which have been underlined?

2 Using the diagram and the information given in the itinerary, write the rest of the advertisement. Remember to link the facts together in a variety of ways.

- what you will do
- what you will see
- visits, cruises, tours
- Visit to China
- architecture, landscape
- how you will travel
- why we recommend this holiday
- where you will stay

3 What part of the itinerary is covered by the introductory paragraph? Use the rest of the itinerary as a framework to complete the article. You should refer to your Vocabulary Resource 6.2, 8.1 and 12.1.

ITINERARY

DAY 1	Depart on non-stop Air China flight to Beijing.
DAY 2	Arrive Beijing and transfer to central 4-star hotel for three nights.
DAYS 3–4	Visit the Forbidden City and the Summer Palace, or day trip to the Great Wall and the valley of the Ming tombs.
DAY 5	Fly to Wuhan and board river vessel for five-night upstream cruise.
DAYS 6–9	Cruise Yangste via Shanshi and ancient city of Janzhou and the famous Three Gorges (total length 310 km).
DAY 10	Arrive Chongquing for city tour and overnight stay.
DAY 11	Fly to Xian and stay two nights grand Castle Hotel.
DAY12	Visit famous Terracotta soldiers, the provincial museum, the wild Goose pagoda and ancient city walls.
DAY 13	Xian to Beijing for two-night stay.
DAY 14	Optional sightseeing.
DAY 15	Depart Beijing.

English in Use

Part 6

Read the article below about the London Underground (the Tube). Choose the best phrases from A–J to fill spaces 1–6. One answer has been given as an example.

UP THE TUBE

TOOTING BEC STATION

Instead of complaining about the Northern Line, we Londoners ought to feel grateful for the tube, the envy of other cities. Liverpool and Newcastle have local lines of a faintly tube-like appearance but they go underground for very short distances, (0) __J__ .

Thirty years ago, my friend Pearl from Peacehaven came up to London (1)____ . She had to be coaxed on to the escalator, and gave little shrieks of delighted horror (2)____ . Inside the train she looked out of the window at blackness in alarm. Like all who gaze through underground windows, she saw not only blackness (3)____ .

When the escalator first began, my family tells me, (4)____ . Hence the unmoveable steps that sometimes run parallel to the moving staircase. My aunt, straight from a village in Poland, was struck with terror at the sight of the escalator, (5)____ . Those were chivalrous times and two London Transport officials heaved her on and held on to her as she screamed, kicked and struggled. I bet they were glad when they reached the top (6)____ .

A   and refused point-blank to ascend

B   for she was a large aunt

C   as if she were on a fairground roller-coaster

D   as there's nothing quite like it

E   but her own reflection

F   many adults were frightened of it

G   but because she was scared

H   and I showed her the sights

I   even though she had made up her mind

J   so I don't think they qualify as tubes

Vocabulary

1 Write 8 sentences using a verb on the left and a noun on the right.

make	a photo
take	experience
hire	a sport
spend	plan
do	an outing
gain	the view
go on	a car
take in	a day

2 An incorrect word has been used in most of the sentences below. Underline the incorrect word and put the correct word at the end of the line. Tick the sentence if it is correct.

1   Children are always told not
   to speak to foreigners.   _____

2   Less people are going on
   exotic holidays this year.   _____

3   It is better to take the motorway
   as the shore road is very busy in
   the summer.   _____

4   Hurry up, we haven't much
   time before the boat leaves.   _____

5   The explorers found the trip
   across the frozen wastes
   completely exhausting.   _____

6   Owen is a sympathetic little
   boy who is very popular with
   his classmates.   _____

7   After studying various historic
   documents they realized the
   building was very old.   _____

8   The trouble with Harry is he
   passes too much time in cafes
   and bars.   _____

English in Use

Part 2

1 Read the magazine article below, ignoring the spaces, and complete the title.

2 Supply the missing words for the article by writing one word in the spaces 1–15. The first one has been done as an example.

THE TRAGEDY

OF _____

They should have been safe. The Titanic's wireless began receiving warnings (0)___*from*___ other ships as early (1)_____ Friday, April 12, to beware of "bergs, growlers and field ice". (2)_____ Sunday the weather had grown chillier and the warnings had increased (3)_____ frequency. (4)_____ the sky was clear and the Atlantic calm as a pond. At 9.20 in the evening, the Titanic's captain, Edward J. Smith, went to bed, (5)_____ left instructions to be roused if the situation (6)_____ "at all doubtful". At (7)_____ the same time, the crow's nest* was ordered to "keep a sharp lookout for ice." But (8)_____ Frederick Fleet and Reginald Lee climbed to their post 40 minutes (9)_____, they had no binoculars. (10)_____ the Titanic's officers did not issue binoculars to the men in the crow's nest is (11)_____ that has never been satisfactorily explained. Forty minutes later, as the Titanic's 46,328 tons bore over the water at (12)_____ than 21 knots, lookout Fleet stared (13)_____ horror at a black phantom on the horizon. This was the ship's doom: (14)_____ a snow-dusted white iceberg, as often imagined, but a dark, colourless hulk. Fleet clanged desperately three times on the crow's nest bell and phoned the ship's bridge: "Iceberg right (15)_____!".

* crow's nest: lookout platform fixed to the highest point of a ship's mast

---

Structure

1 Underline and identify the type of clause in sentences 1–12 below. Choose from: defining relative, non-defining relative, noun, or adverb. In each case say what the clause adds to the sentence.

1 The seagulls, which had been swooping over the quay side and snatching our sandwiches, had disappeared out to sea.

2 It wasn't long before the officer who was on duty during the storm was allowed to leave the ship.

3 The travellers wanted to know why the train was late.

4 They soon found out that the hotel had been over-charging them.

5 The ferries whose crews were not on strike took the stranded passengers back to the mainland.

6 As soon as the train drew into the station she ran to get on as if her life depended on it.

7 He was so pleased with his holiday that he decided to book exactly the same one for the following year.

8 What she wanted to know was how long it would take to get to Scotland by car.

9 The guests complained to the manager that the swimming pool had been out of action since the day they arrived.

10 The teenagers had climbed to the top of the cliff where they hoped they would be spotted by a rescue party.

11 The group that had remained at the safari lodge were rewarded with a wonderful chance to see the lions at close quarters.

12 Despite being cold and hungry the skiers insisted on taking the lift to the top once more.

2 Reread the article about homeopathic medicines at the beginning of this unit. Underline the clauses and decide what they add to each paragraph.

3 Here is paragraph 9 rewritten with the clauses removed. What is the effect?

The kit continued its journey for a full six months. Some things worked and others didn't. This entire area of medicine warrants careful consideration. I am a person with no experience in this field and I have a sceptical outlook. I was still able to find genuinely beneficial remedies. My scepticism has been tempered and my knowledge broadened. I have an open mind about homeopathy. Some medical doctors do not.

9 Rites and Rituals

Reading

1 Quickly read the article *Playing with fire*. Can you name two religions common in Japan (other than Christianity)? What aspects of Japanese life are associated with them?

Playing with fire

Beth Nicholls glimpses the many faces of Japan as she finds herself caught up in the festival spirit

A

Normally the tiny village of Kurama in the North of Kyoto is a peaceful place where visitors relax in the natural hot springs, or follow the shrine trail far on up the mountain. But today was different. Today was the annual 'Hi Matsuri' (Fire Festival) and the stories of blazing torches and glowing skies had lured others too. Lots of others. The streets were alive as dusk fell and the darkness crept in. All the villagers had opened their traditional houses, and had each lit a small fire near the entrance way. The chanting had begun. The stamping followed. Men beclothed in little more than G-strings and leaf mini-skirts started pacing the streets, slowly at first, getting accustomed to the weight of the 15ft torch on their shoulders. Small children clutching their own brands followed in their fathers' footsteps, their proud smiles revealed by the dancing flames. The soft chant increased in volume and intensity until the words became a war cry filling the raw night air. Through the streets they marched, past the crowds and up the front steps of the shrine, on a mission intended to guide the gods on their way around our world.

B

Part of the fascination with Japan is that its people have so many faces. The scantily clad torch-bearer by night is probably a blue-suited *salariman* by day, the average Japanese person's life being a continual fluctuation between the extremes of contemporary and tradition. Much of this tradition, as all over the world, has its roots in deity worship, and Japan in particular sees the thread of religion tightly woven into everyday existence. The Japanese are exposed to Buddhism, but also to Shinto (the religion indigenous to Japan), to the moral codes of Confucianism, and even, to a more limited extent, to Christianity. If, during their lifetime, a Japanese person had taken part in Shinto festivals, had a Shinto or Christian wedding, and had lived day-to-day by the teachings of Confucius, and then had a Buddhist funeral, few eyebrows would be raised.

C

Essentially harmonious, side by side they educate in matters of the spiritual kind. Festivals are predominantly Shinto and are generally seen as opportunities for locals to dance, wear bizarre clothes and drink copious amounts of local *sake* (rice wine). Such festivals go on, somewhere in Japan, almost every day. Whereas Shinto finds its home in shrines, Buddhism favours temples, and there the atmosphere tends to be somewhat more calming.

D

As for the Buddhist monks (*obosan*), they can often be heard walking the streets of an evening, chanting in deep, haunting tones whilst holding a collecting bowl in an outstretched hand. These monks have a habit of turning up where you'd least expect them, as I recently discovered. Shaved, head held high, back stiffened and with purpose in his eyes, the obosan stared straight ahead of him. With peculiar wooden sandals on his feet and a conical straw hat in his hands, even the way his navy robe fell about him described an air of assuredness, grace and wisdom. Then he hopped on the bus.

E

Any guide book on Japan will go to great lengths to describe the country and its people as a nation of contrasts, but only because it is a hard point to ignore. I don't know how I'd expect the Buddhist monk to get to work – maybe I had a dream-like image of him just meditating by a small waterfall, pausing only to strike the temple gong, with no regard to office hours or public transport. And maybe it was in that same temple that I assumed the possessionless monk would find his home. But seeing him on the bus made me wake up to my romantic vision, and simultaneously fired off a stream of observations about the blatant contrasts in this country – my paper-windowed, *tatami*-floored room with its state-of-the-art TV; the kimono-clad woman with her mobile phone; the old lady bent double praying alone in the small street shrine, oblivious to the hideous silver *pachinko* parlour overshadowing her. Each one of these things is as true a reflection of today's Japanese society as the next.

F

A haven for culture vultures, Kyoto is the ancient capital of Japan and it was from here that I based my explorations. Surrounded on three sides by mountains and with over 2000 temples and shrines, the city provides the Japan that foreigners dream of – *geisha* girls, raked sand gardens and stunning old buildings. Unfortunately at the more famous sites you are likely to see more of chattering schoolgirls and the flags of Japanese tour guides than of what you actually came to see. But if you go early and listen carefully, you can smell fresh incense and hear the monks being called to morning prayer and meditation. And whilst listening you can ponder whether their bald heads get cold in winter, how they manage to walk in those shoes, or where they actually keep their bus tickets.

G

As for the geisha girls, they are the epitome of everything traditionally Japanese. Literally 'accomplished in the arts', the *maikos* (trainees) and *geikos* (fully fledged geisha) learn age old skills such as dancing, *ikebana* (flower arranging) and the tea ceremony (preparation of frothy green tea which is served with bean cakes, very slowly and gracefully). They are phenomenally expensive to 'hire' for an evening – far beyond the average individual's budget, and are usually employed for office functions. Once widespread, the geisha community is today limited to Kyoto and parts of Tokyo. To follow the tripping step of a maiko through the streets of Gion, Kyoto's entertainment district, is to take a step back in time. Past wooden-fronted restaurants with red paper lanterns swinging in the breeze, the white-faced immaculate geisha walks on, pigeon toed, through the narrow streets to work. Same make-up, same hair, same kimono, same job, same streets as generations of geisha before her.

H

Traditional villages grew up deep in the mountains and religious fastidiousness guided the lives of the Japanese for many years. The festivals and rituals that survive today display but a handful of the superstitions and beliefs of the nation centuries ago. Though it is easy to get swept off your feet by the romance of the country, the images of old are rapidly fading. The *samurai* have gone and the geisha are going. Japan, the land of the Rising Sun, is being swept behind a cloud of hi-tech industry and visions of the future. But if you look carefully, very carefully, you will see a patch of blue sky.

1,125 words

2   Scan the article again and identify which sections (A–H) refer to which topics. Some sections may be chosen more than once.

images of the old and new	1 _____	2 _____	3 _____
religion as part of life	4 _____	5 _____	
some traditional roles continue	6 _____	7 _____	
a city of temples and shrines	8 _____		
festivals are fun	9 _____	10 _____	
traditional rituals survive	11 _____	12 _____	13 _____
the ancient culture is dying	14 _____		
a surprising monk	15 _____		

3 This article has come from a travel magazine. Look at the features of this style of writing on page 114 of the Student's Book.

4 Look at each paragraph and decide which of these features are used. See if you can work out the organization of the article by looking at what links each paragraph.

Vocabulary

1 Find these collocates in the article and say what they are describing and what they mean:

copious amounts   scantily clad   tightly woven

2 Underline the collocates (which also appear in this article), in the sentences below and make sure you understand what they mean.

a   To a limited extent the Japanese are also exposed to Christianity.

b   Nobody will raise an eyebrow if someone takes part in Shinto festivals but marries in a Christian church.

c   The monk held his collecting bowl in an outstretched hand.

d   The city is full of temples so it is a good place for culture vultures.

e   To visit Kyoto is like taking a step back in time.

f   Evidence of Japan's ancient culture is fading rapidly.

3 Use the collocates in 1 and 2 to complete the following sentences.

1   The beaches were crowded with _____ _____ teenagers enjoying the sea and sun.

2   Hardly anybody would _____ _____ if you didn't get married in a church.

3   A city like Florence is always full of _____ _____ determined to see the sights.

4   After a day in the Australian bush we showered and settled down to drink _____ _____ of cold beer.

5   The house was in its original state and as you went through the front door you took

_____.

6   _____ the people celebrate Christmas and New Year.

7   The beggar stood at the bottom of the escalator with _____.

8   In the market peasants were selling baskets made of _____ reeds.

English in Use

Part 6

1 Skim read this extract from a magazine article ignoring the spaces. What do you think is meant by 'life below stairs'?

SERVING PETWORTH

Diana Owen dishes up a feast of information on life below stairs in 19th century West Sussex.

The kitchens at Petworth House in West Sussex opened to the public for the first time in 1995 and resulted in a flood of interest in the lives and times of the servants at Petworth.

(0) __J__ Petworth was served by an army of staff housed largely in the purpose-built separate Servants' Block. (1)_____ arranged in a strict hierarchy with the House Steward and upper servants at the top. The House Steward was a 'gentleman' who did not wear livery and who lived in some style, maintaining his own dining room for entertaining visiting senior staff. (2)_____ the running of the house, employing staff and paying bills and wages.

(3)_____ was her great bunch of keys, and this busy lady was in charge of up to twelve housemaids

2 Now complete the extract by choosing the best phrases from A–J to fill spaces 1–6. Remember there are more phrases to choose from than there are spaces. One answer has been given as an example.

A The Housekeeper's badge of office

B Always addressed as

C In the 1870s and 1880s the chef

D The other upper servants were

E He was assisted by

F This bustling community

G He was responsible for

H There were 35 indoor staff

I She also ran the china and linen stores

J Like all great houses

and daily help such as extra cleaners and seamstresses. (4)_____ and undertook the organisation of the laundry. (5)_____ 'Mrs' whether married or not as a mark of respect, the Housekeeper had her own sitting room and large bedroom.

(6)_____, dedicated to maintaining the highest standards in cuisine, housekeeping and all other aspects of domestic service, was a vital component of 'the Family'.

Vocabulary

1 In this article you came across the verbs *resulted in* and *served by*. Here are some other verbs which combine with *in* and *by*. Choose an appropriate form of one of the verbs to complete the sentences below.

> assist
> stand   in
> live   by
> join

1 We were _____ our efforts to get the car started by Henry.

2 They were soon _____ other guests attending the same party.

3 He was asked to _____ for the lead singer who had been delayed by traffic.

4 She always tries to _____ the principles of her religion.

5 Although Hannah was very shy she soon _____ the game.

6 John _____ fear of his secret being discovered.

7 If they try to make Ann resign, we'll _____ her.

8 _____ the weather, the yacht crossed the Atlantic in record time.

2 **Related parts of speech.** Use a dictionary to complete these sets of related words. Remember that the related forms may not be consecutive entries.

NOUN	ADJECTIVE	VERB
entertainment	entertaining	entertain
_____	_____	organize
servant	_____	_____
_____	arranged	_____
_____	_____	marry
_____	_____	dedicate
army	_____	_____
_____	separate	_____

Writing

1 Read the first and final paragraphs of an article about parties. What is the writer's view about parties in the fifties? What links the two paragraphs together in terms of content and structure?

First paragraph

In the fifties there was a great deal of emphasis on grand parties and grand dressing. We had lively parties in the South of France, impromptu parties in the Village. But whether a party was on Eighth Street or Fifth Avenue, people made an effort. All the women would be resplendent in their French dresses, there would be music lingering in the background and somebody or other from Hollywood would get up and entertain.

Final paragraph

Oddly enough, I don't remember a bad party during that era. It was an age where you could still be impressed; you weren't jaded. A party was an occasion, and you were seeing things on a grand scale that you hadn't seen before.

2 Read this advertisement for a writing competition in a magazine aimed at young adults.

When was your most memorable party?

Write and tell us about the wildest or the most glamorous party you have ever been to. Or tell us about that ghastly surprise 'do' that went so terribly wrong or the one you went to when you hadn't been invited!

We will print the best six articles in our Winter issue and each winner will receive tickets for a ball at the Dorchester Hotel in London.

3 Choose one of the opening paragraphs below and finish the article in about 200 words. Remember to link your final paragraph to the first paragraph.

A

The most glamorous party I ever went to was given by the parents of a friend of mine. It was her eighteenth birthday and she had asked if it could be held on a boat. Obviously her parents must have had quite a bit of money because it wasn't just any old boat They hired a …

B

I don't enjoy surprises very much, even nice ones, and a surprise party is to me a refined sort of torture. On this occasion I was completely unprepared. In fact I had forgotten that it was our anniversary and had decided to have a hot bath and an early night. Unfortunately that was not how things turned out. I got home from work rather late that evening …

C

When my brother told me that the party to celebrate his wife's latest book was that evening I could only imagine that they must have forgotten to invite me. Not wishing to disappoint them I threw on something warm and comfortable, as their flat is always so cold, and drove over. I knocked on the door and my sister-in-law opened it …

Structure

1 Look at this example from the article about Petworth House:

The kitchens at Petworth House in West Sussex opened to the public for the first time in 1995…

What form of the verb is used? Why is *for* used rather than *since*?

Complete the following sentences by supplying a suitable form of the verb: present perfect simple, present perfect continuous, simple past and *for* or *since* if needed.

1 I'm awfully tired. I _____ (not/have) a day off _____ over a week.

2 George _____ (want) to use the swimming pool ever _____ (build).

3 The teenagers _____ (stop) dancing when the neighbours _____ (object) to the noise.

4 We _____ (try) to telephone you _____ days but you never _____ (seem to be) in.

5 My father _____ (tell) me last night that he _____ (know) about the problem _____ years.

6 There _____ (be) plenty of water in the reservoir _____ the water company _____(mend) the pipes.

7 She _____ (complain) to her manager because her colleagues _____ (tease) her _____ she _____ (promote) above them.

8 _____ weeks the team _____ (train) every evening and _____ (reward) by a spectacular win in their first away game.

2 Read this paragraph and underline the future perfect verbs. Decide whether the verbs are like those in A1, 2 or 3 on page 123 of your Student's Book.

In two years' time Matthew will have left school and found a job. He'll have been living on his own and finding out how tough it can be. His parents will have accepted that he is not going to live by their rules. However, they will have spent a good deal of time worrying about him, too.

3 Read the article below, then supply the missing words using *since, for, yet, still, long* or the verb given in brackets in a perfect tense.

The dominant tribal group of the Annapurna range are the Gurungs, a hardy people renowned for their loyalty and fierceness. The Gurungs have (1)_____ been recruited by the British Army to serve in its Gurkha regiments, and many former soldiers (2)_____ (go back) to their villages bringing wealth and knowledge. (3)_____ returning they have opened up bhattis, tea houses-cum-lodges, to cater for the ever-growing number of visitors to the region. It is the bhattis and the friendly people running them that (4)_____ (help) make this Nepal's most popular trekking route. Crime is (5)_____ a rarity, despite the incredible disparity in wealth between these people and the visitors passing through. (6)_____ with the popularity of this region come intense ecological pressures. More than 95% of Nepal's energy requirements are met by the burning of wood and (7)_____ many years this (8)_____ (mean) indiscriminate felling of trees. The ultimate casualty (9)_____ (be) Nepal's rhododendron forests. Until recently, as much as 3% of the country's total forest area (10)_____ _____ (clear) annually.

Reading

1 The title of the article is *An Overshadowed Childhood*. Skim read the article, ignoring the missing paragraphs, and decide what the title is referring to.

2 Now read paragraphs A–G. Six of these paragraphs fit into the gaps in the article. There is one extra paragraph which doesn't fit anywhere. Insert the paragraphs into gaps 1–6. Remember to look out for linking devices.

An Overshadowed Childhood

I can still recall the pain and intensity of the flare-ups in most of my joints during the early stages of my arthritis from the age of two onwards. I would call for my bewildered parents during the night to "unlock my legs". They used a rota system to look after me, and their patience was endless.

(1)____

I constantly complained when any walking was to be done. My mother would regularly march me round to our doctor, looking for reassurance. That always ended up with a smack because of Mum's frustration at being told there was nothing wrong with me other than I was a spoilt, miserable child.

(2)____

I was in hospital for a month. My brother and sister were not allowed to visit me, which made me fretful and unsettled. I was diagnosed with what was then known as Still's disease.

(3)____

Much of my play was solitary and hospital-inspired. I would give my mother strict orders to collect any spare wax left over when it was peeled from my joints. Mum would then boil up the wax when we arrived home. I would lay all my dolls out and wax their joints, putting them through what I had to endure every day. I also used to pretend to take blood from my dolls' ears and make them yelp just like I did.

(4)____

I hated to be seen in the chair, and if I saw anyone I recognized I used to turn my hat back to front to hide my face. I forgot about my little stick legs, which gave me away. I wanted my knee-length boots to fit snugly around my calves like those of other girls, but there was so much spare room. I painstakingly lined the insides of my boots with foam draught excluder to make them fit snugly.

(5)____

I eventually attended secondary school full-time from 11 to 16. It was quite a tough inner-city girls' school. Many of the children had very serious social problems but I never experienced any discrimination.

(6)____

I was not unhappy at school, as I was always surrounded by caring friends, but I could never lose the feeling of being different.

A

I went to junior school part-time from the age of eight to eleven. I went to school in the mornings and then the hospital in the afternoon.

B

I cannot remember objecting to the endless blood tests, X-rays, hot salt baths, wax baths, sunlight treatment and intensive physiotherapy but I recall absolutely dreading the scales coming out each week, not because I minded being weighed, but because we were all weighed in the same room, naked. I felt so humiliated even at four-and-a-half.

C

There wasn't much I could do about the diagnosis so I decided I would have to teach myself to walk again. It was a long and painful process.

D

I never returned to my infant school. I had a teacher who came to my house for two hours a week and set me basic maths and English work. My mum was my main teacher. She would push me, in a renovated wheelchair, to the local hospital, each afternoon, for physiotherapy. My three-year-old brother would pedal alongside on his bicycle.

E

Some of the really 'hard cases' were protective of me. They would fight over whose turn it was to carry my bag or bring me a chair to sit on. I was always asked to keep the score for netball and rounders while sitting at the edge of the pitch looking on.

F

Once during PE at infant school we were told to skip to the music. As I couldn't move my hips enough to skip properly, I skipped in my own fashion. The teacher corrected me and then proceeded to take my hand and make me skip, slapping my bottom in time to the music. Each slap was meant to make me lift my leg and hop. Tears were streaming down my face. Eventually I could not take any more and I was sent home from school and my mother, no longer willing to accept the opinion of our doctor, demanded that I see a specialist immediately. I was admitted to hospital the same day.

G

I can remember when my aunt used to swing me by the arms – making me fly like an aeroplane just as she had done for my brother and sister. Not wanting to be left out, I wanted to do the same – but I screamed rather than laughed like the other two.

Vocabulary

1 The following verbs and prepositions appear in the article. Find them in the text and check you understand what they mean.

march round   boil up   lay out   forget about
come out   surrounded by   look after
do about   fight over   look on   stream down

2 Insert suitable verbs from the list above into sentences 1–10.

1   The decision has already been taken so there is nothing to be _____ it.

2   At high tide the castle is _____ water and can only be reached by boat.

3   There was no clean drinking water so we had to _____ large saucepans of water on the stove.

4   She _____ her clothes on the bed before packing them into the suitcase.

5   As he was the eldest it was his responsibility to _____ the younger children.

6   When I stood up I saw I had cut my knee and blood was _____ my leg.

7   As soon as I leave the office I can _____ the work and just relax.

8   After the election the new Prime Minister _____ of his office and spoke to the crowds.

9   We should try to come to some agreement on the big issues rather than _____ small matters.

10   The two men stood in the road and shouted at each other whilst a small group of people just _____.

English in Use

Part 4

1 Read the article below ignoring the gaps. What aspect of mental health care is the writer unhappy about?

   a   the use of certain drugs on mental patients

   b   the way patients are neglected by the medical profession

   c   the lack of involvement by patients in their treatment

2 Insert the correct form of the words given in capitals below into each of the gaps.

In Search of the Right Balance

Professionals in the mental health field develop (0)_____*clinical*_____ skills and theoretical (1)_____ in order to be helpful in some way. I have never doubted the (2)_____ of drugs to treat mental illness but I am concerned that by (3)_____ giving priority to medical treatment we neglect the importance of (4)_____ self-management and the personal choice of the patient. We must show a (5)_____ to helping patients understand their experiences. It is (6)_____ to rely on an approach which regards medical (7)_____ as the primary focus, and caring for the patient's social and emotional needs as an afterthought.

---

  0   CLINIC
  1   PREFER
  2   USE
  3   CONTINUE
  4   INDEPENDENCE
  5   COMMIT
  6   SATISFY
  7   INTERVENE

Writing

> You have read the extract from the article entitled *In Search of the Right Balance* and a letter written about the article by another reader of the magazine. You do not agree with what has been said in the letter and so you have decided to write to the magazine putting your views about the care of the mentally ill.

1 Read the article again and the letter below. Match the negative points in the letter to relevant parts of the article.

2 Highlight any other points in the letter and the article which you can agree with or argue against. Remember you can add points of your own as long as you have covered the issues raised in the letter and the article.

Dear Sir

I read the article in your magazine last week about how mentally ill people should decide how they should be treated. I find this idea is very frightening and potentially dangerous for the community. I believe that if you are suffering from a serious mental illness you are not in a fit condition to make decisions about how you are treated. The best thing for these people, and the rest of us, is for them to be kept in secure hospitals where they can be treated by doctors with appropriate drugs or whatever is necessary.

There is too much talk nowadays about the rights of certain individuals who do not fit into our society. We should be concentrating on the rights of the majority of law-abiding and sane individuals before we start to worry about the 'rights' of people who might be a danger to others if they are able to choose what sort of treatment they can have.

Yours faithfully
W. F. Wilson

---

3 Here are the opening and closing paragraphs of your letter. Write the remaining part of the letter in about 100 words. You need to:

a   decide on the points you want to make.

b   remember not to lift actual phrases from the article or the letter.

c   check your writing carefully.

Introductory paragraph

Dear Sir

I read the article "In Search of the Right Balance" in the July edition of your magazine and the letter from W.F. Wilson in this month's edition. I found the article both reasonable and well-argued in its attempt to put forward the need to ensure that even the mentally ill should be involved in the decisions surrounding their care. I agree that all patients, and in particular those suffering from mental illness, must be treated with dignity. It is so easy to forget that someone who may be acting strangely must still be regarded as a human being.

Concluding paragraph

In conclusion, I would add that, in my experience, all but the most seriously ill mental patient can gain enormously from being given some power over their lives. It is the professionals who care for them who must be given the responsibility of involving the patients but it is the rest of us in society who must support them in this process.

Yours faithfully

English in Use

Part 5

Read the following letter from a social worker to a colleague asking for some advice about a client. Use the information in it to complete the numbered gaps in the formal case study notes. Use no more than two words for each gap. The words you need do not occur in the letter.

Dear Janet

I've recently started visiting this client and I'd be grateful for some advice.

A.J. is 23 and has had arthritis since she was five. It mostly affects her joints and so she's severely disabled. She has to have help with everything. She needs a wheelchair and hasn't worked since she left school. She doesn't get out much. Her parents gave up work to look after her, so they have to live on state benefits.

A.J. has become the centre of family life which means that her two sisters may not be getting enough attention. One of them thinks that A.J. is too dependent on her parents. I think she means there is something wrong with the relationship between A.J. and her parents. It's clear to me that her illness has had an enormous effect on the family…

CASE STUDY

A.J., now 23, developed Systemic Onset J.C.A., which affected most of the synovial joints, at the age of five. She was (0)_____ *left* _____ with severe disability and needs help with virtually all activities of daily living. She is a wheelchair (1)_____ and has been unemployed since finishing full-time education. She rarely (2)_____ the house. Her parents are full-time (3)_____, both having given up work to look after their daughter. As a result their only income is state benefits. A.J.'s illness seems to (4)_____ her at the centre of family life, perhaps at the (5)_____ her two siblings. One of her (6)_____ feels that A.J. is now so dependent on her parents that she will not (7)_____ when they can no longer look after her. She (8)_____ that the relationship is dysfunctional. (9)_____ the disease appears to have played a (10)_____ in the development of this family's dynamics.

Structure

1 Which words in the following phrases from the articles in this unit are gerunds and which are present participles?

a   when any walking was to be done

b   at being told there was nothing wrong with me

c   putting them through what I had to endure

d   tears were streaming down my face

e   surrounded by caring friends

f   no longer willing to accept the opinion

g   I cannot remember objecting to

h   the feeling of being different

i   I recall absolutely dreading

j   caring for the patient's social and emotional needs

k   while sitting at the edge of the pitch looking on

l   giving priority to medical treatment

m   slapping my bottom in time to the music

n   I've recently started visiting this patient

o   having given up work

2 Insert suitable present participles into the following sentences formed from the verbs in the list below. In which sentences are they used as adjectives?

send   care   read   collect   visit
worry   amuse   try

1   After _____ the article she decided to see what she could do to help.

2   As the rains failed again this year the situation is _____.

3   When _____ sponsorship money door-to-door make sure you have some identification with you.

4   Although the story was _____, I didn't feel like laughing.

5   He was advised against _____ the country due to the outbreak of civil war.

6   He was captured whilst _____ to swim across the river.

7   The minister is often photographed with refugees and this gives people the impression she is a _____ person.

8   When _____ a donation please remember that only cheques and banker's orders are accepted.

3 Insert a gerund or an infinitive of the verb in brackets into the following sentences. In which sentences can you use either a gerund or an infinitive?

1   Jenny can't afford _____ (buy) shoes for her children.

2   Many people dislike _____ (give) money to people begging on the streets.

3   It seems _____ (be) more common for old people to live on their own in Britain.

4   The social worker suggested _____ (look) at his report again before making any decisions.

5   We should all begin _____ (care) about the environment more.

6   The old man refused _____ (come) inside even though it was freezing outside.

7   Some organizations continue _____ (donate) large sums to charity, despite inflation.

8   He can't remember _____ (spend) so much money on clothes before.

Today's World

Reading

1 Skim read the article without looking at the questions. What is the difference between the American and the British view of space aliens?

THE *Alien* HALF-CENTURY

FIFTY YEARS AGO – in June 1947 – an American businessman named Kenneth Arnold was flying his private aircraft near Mount Rainier in Washington State when he saw a group of strange objects flying in the sky. He said that they 'skipped like saucers across the water'. News agencies immediately coined the expression 'flying saucers' and pretty soon strange objects in the sky were being reported from all over America and, to a lesser extent, from other countries. Right from the start the most popular theory was that they were spacecraft from another planet.

What Arnold actually saw, if anything, has never been established. He reported several more sightings in future years, which makes him sound more than a little dubious. Yet he has launched the greatest myth of the age.

Nothing in a present scientific picture of the universe excludes the possibility of intelligent extraterrestrial life, but there is a complete absence of evidence for it. There is nothing that we can look at and analyse, only strange tales. There are some interesting scientific arguments which suggest that life must be very rare and that we may even be alone. Yet this is not a popular view and nobody wants to hear about it.

America is the world centre of the UFO cult, although there is an amiable and in some ways more sensible British offshoot. Fashions change in space aliens as in everything else. In the 1950s and 60s the space aliens were thought to be benevolent and worried in case the human race destroyed itself with nuclear weapons.

Carl Jung in his *Flying Saucers: A Modern Myth of Things Seen in the Sky* (1959) considered that flying saucers reflected 'a religious vacuum at the heart of modern man'. They had come, Jung argued, at a time of general anxiety coupled with growing religious doubt and expressed the desire for some external power to save us. Jung very likely got close to the heart of the matter, even if the aliens are not seen as saviours any more. In our darker and more paranoid time the aliens are far from benevolent and are frequently abducting people, especially bored and lonely housewives, and carrying out unpleasant experiments on them.

Of course the US government was held to be hiding things from the start. Probably the US air force made a mistake in setting up Project Blue Book in 1948 to look into flying saucer reports. It was all quite innocent, but it created the ineradicable impression that the air force knew there was something going on. Actually the air force had no idea what was going on in 1947, but by 1950 had come to the conclusion that there was no great flying saucer mystery.

For example, the alleged Roswell incident took place in 1947 when a farmer found some debris – probably from a secret military balloon – on his farm near Roswell, New Mexico. There was quite a song and dance for a while about a 'crashed saucer', but it was soon forgotten.

Thirty years later, however, Roswell was being cited as evidence of alien visitation and official deceit. In the Roswell case – which has been the subject now of half a dozen books and one feature film – aliens and their spaceship are alleged to have been spirited away and hidden by the air force. American space technology, however, has a very lucid history from the space shuttle back to the German V2s acquired in 1945. It would have been different if they had had access to alien technology.

At the root of conspiracism lies the belief that the world is not a chapter of accidents but that, on the contrary, everything is under control and going according to plan – somebody's plan. In America such journals as *Critique*, published in California, and *Conspiracy Tracker*, published in New Jersey, maintain a running commentary on the various conspiracies.

In Britain the atmosphere is far less fevered. Researchers such as Jenny Randles, Hilary Evans and Paul Deveraux seem a touch uncritical at times, but they inhabit the same universe of the mind as do the rest of us. UFOs may not be from another planet but in general, space aliens are not much fancied in Britain and British ufologists are more inclined to put UFO reports into the category of the paranormal, along with telepathy, precognition and ghosts. Sceptics will certainly agree that UFO stories – and all that we can examine of UFOs are the stories – should be put into that department.

Most of us at this point would be happy to shut the door quietly and silently make off. My own Boring Theory of History (BTH) states that the true explanation of any mystery is the most tedious explanation consistent with the facts. In the case of the UFOs the BTH predicts that when you have eliminated regular aircraft, irregular aircraft, balloons, the planet Venus, lunatics, liars and film producers and other conventional categories, what you will be left with is nothing.

840 words

---

2 Read through the questions and options before reading the article again and then answer questions 1–6.

1 Why was Kenneth Arnold's experience in 1947 so significant?

A The objects he saw looked like saucers.
B The Press believed his account.
C His was the first recorded sighting.
D Other people were able to confirm his story.

2 What does science tell us about the possibility of intelligent life on other planets?

A There is some evidence that it exists.
B There is some evidence that Earth is the only inhabited planet.
C There is no possibility whatsoever.
D There are one or two planets which need further investigation.

3 What was Jung's view of flying saucers?

A They represent a need in people to believe in something.
B They are evidence that there is a God who cares for us.
C They are a symptom of the darker side of our nature.
D They are only seen by those who are mentally disturbed.

4 What did people think about aliens in the 1950s and 1960s.

A They were a passing fashion.
B They wanted to destroy us.
C They wanted to make friends with us.
D They wanted to protect us from ourselves.

5 What made people think that the US airforce was involved in a conspiracy?

A The setting up of Project Blue Book.
B The development of the American space technology programme.
C The disappearance of the secret military balloon in 1947.
D The TV series based on the Roswell incident.

6 What does the writer think about UFOs?

A They are a paranormal experience.
B They can be explained by ordinary events.
C They were invented by American journalists.
D They do not interest him very much.

3 Like the article in Unit 11 of the Student's Book, *The True Value of Age*, this article is similar in some ways to a report but is written in an informal style for the general reader. Find examples from the article of the following:

a Giving an opinion.

b Speculating.

c Reporting what someone has said.

Vocabulary

1 The expressions *carrying out* and *make off* appear in the article above. Find them in the text and decide what they mean. Here are some other verbs which combine with *off* and *out*. Choose an appropriate form of one of them to complete the sentences below.

> miss
>
> run   out
>
> give   off
>
> take

1 If the students aren't invited to the seminar they will feel they are _____.

2 We'd better go shopping soon as we've _____ of everything.

3 The cheese was _____ an awful smell so we threw it away.

4 The dentist had to _____ several of my teeth.

5 Unfortunately his name was _____ the list so he didn't come.

6 When the alarm sounded the intruders _____.

7 Her patience eventually _____ and she shouted at them to keep quiet.

8 The plane _____ despite the fog.

2 Find these phrases in the article and match them to the best meanings, choosing from 1–6. Then find phrases in the article for the two extra meanings.

a   right from the start

b   coupled with

c   the heart of the matter

d   come to the conclusion

1   a little bit

2   decided

3   a fuss

4   together with

5   immediately

6   the real reason

English in Use

Part 2

1 The expression 'Your life in their hands' is sometimes used to describe the work of surgeons. Read the article below. In what sense is the title 'Life in Their Hands' suitable?

2 Supply the missing words by writing one word in spaces 1–15. The first one has been done for you as an example.

Life in Their Hands

When I first heard that Japan's latest craze was a computer pet you can keep in your pocket, I scoffed (0)____*at*____ the idea. I mean, (1)_____ on earth could get attached to a silly egg-shaped game on a key-ring? But the makers were (2)_____ to a good thing. So good, in fact, that they didn't (3)_____ bother to advertise. (4)_____ no time, 'Tamagotchis' were selling (5)_____ hot cakes. Originally priced at (6)_____ than $20 each, they were soon changing hands on the black market for $800. So, naturally, when a friend of (7)_____ gave me a Tamagotchi, my first thought was how much I could sell it (8)_____ . But (9)_____ I could even imagine my future riches, my friend had set the thing going and suddenly I was a parent (10)_____ a piece of blue transparent plastic. It didn't take (11)_____ for the magnitude of my responsibility to sink in. The Tamagotchi starts (12)_____ a pulsating egg on the screen. (13)_____ five minutes it hatches into a demanding chick, which wants to be fed, played with, and have (14)_____ droppings cleared away regularly. (15)_____ this is done with a series of bleeps and squeaks via three little buttons.

Vocabulary

Read through the paragraphs on page 141 of the Student's Book. The sentences below are more informal ways of expressing some of the same ideas. Complete the sentences using the words in the list. Only use each pair of words once.

think that   have got   just like   killed off
can make   such long   best places   by using
says that   easily solve

1 A recent survey _____ 60% of Masai children _____ trachoma.

2 They _____ the Scottish cliffs are the _____ for huge wind turbines.

3 The marine toad has _____ many local species of lizards and snakes.

4 A turbine can improve the environment _____ a beautiful statue _____ it more attractive.

5 You could _____ the problem _____ an empty tin with a hole in the bottom.

6 The plant has _____ roots it can absorb moisture deep in the ground.

Writing

1 Read this writing task. What is the purpose of the leaflet?

> GUEST is a national organization in your country established to help adult international students feel at home and to promote international friendship. GUEST needs more volunteers to share a weekend or longer with an international student. You have been asked to design a leaflet informing people about the organization and encouraging them to offer their services.

2 Read the partially completed leaflet below. Judging by the headings, what would GUEST volunteers need to know?

GIVE A WELCOME TO INTERNATIONAL STUDENTS

Could you invite an international student to your home for a weekend or a few days at holiday times?

GUEST is a national organization..............

The STUDENTS come from..................

What we ask you to offer:
Please treat them just like a member of your family.....

What your student will give you:
Our students are not well-off so they cannot pay you for their stay. However, they................

What our students say:
Aneka from Poland writes: "It was a really lovely time. We spent it cooking, chatting and laughing together...."

If you are interested:

3 What register do you think you should use, given the purpose of the leaflet and its target readership?

4 Look at the headings and decide what are the main messages you want to get across. Then complete the leaflet in about 150 words. Check your final answer carefully.

English in Use

Part 3

In most lines of the following text, there is either a spelling or a punctuation error. For each numbered line 1–17, write the correctly spelled word(s) or show the correct punctuation next to the line. The exercise begins with two examples.

Picture it: your cruising in virtual silence above the Grand Canyon
in a flying saucer. You can just make out a faint whirring noise
if you listen carefully enough. Don't worry you haven't been
abducted by alians – this is a glimpse into the near future,
acording to Michael Walden. He's the boss of LTAS (Lighter Than
Air Solar) Corporation of Nevada, an he's been building airships
for years. Now he reckons that the tecknologies needed to make
them commercially viable have finally caught up with his idea.
The almost silently, lighter-than-air saucers will be powered
by arrays of solar panels. Panorama 360° windows in the cabin
ensure obstructed views and make the saucer absolutely perfect
for sightseeing tours. But there are times when a flying saucer
brings unforeseen dangers that have nothing to do with the usually
snags associated with aircraft trials Walden tells the sad tale of
when LTAS was involved with a project with Spacial of Mexico
to build a 33m-diametre saucer. Following minor engine problems
in 1990, it's pilot made a soft, emergency landing near a remote
village in Mexico. But when the locale inhabitants saw the huge
saucer descending silently, they panic.

0	_you're_
0	✓
1	_____
2	_____
3	_____
4	_____
5	_____
6	_____
7	_____
8	_____
9	_____
10	_____
11	_____
12	_____
13	_____
14	_____
15	_____
16	_____
17	_____

Structure

1 Read this example of the third conditional and answer the questions.

If the US air force hadn't set up Project Blue Book, there wouldn't have been so much suspicion about their involvement in a cover-up.

a Did the US air force set up Project Blue Book?

b Was there any suspicion about a cover-up?

2 Complete the following conditional sentences using the verbs in brackets. Which of them are examples of the third conditional?

1 If Kenneth Arnold _____ (fly) his private aircraft near Mount Rainier in June 1947, we might never _____ (hear) of Flying Saucers.

2 American space technology would have been different if they _____ (have access) to alien technology.

3 Unless you can be bothered to look after it night and day you _____ (buy) a Tamagotchi.

4 Supposing, however, you _____ (give) this little pulsating egg, _____ (let) it die?

5 Provided you _____ (offer) the students their own bedrooms we _____ (be) entirely satisfied.

6 If the students _____ (tell) us they weren't coming we _____ (warn) you.

3 Which of the sentences in 2 contain mixed (second and third) conditionals?

4 Complete the following with the verbs in brackets to form sentences containing second and third conditionals.

1 If work on the dam _____ (begin) on time , it _____ (finish) by now.

2 If the project _____ (improved) the environment significantly, people _____ (object) to paying for it.

3 If Sophie _____ (have) cosmetic surgery, she _____ (feel) much better about the shape of her nose now.

4 If I _____ (know) about the company's difficulties, I _____ (agree) to work for them.

5 If the marine toad _____ _____ (introduce) into Australia, native species of wildlife _____ _____ (survive) in greater numbers.

6 If the politicians _____ (allowed) wind turbines to be built, most of them _____ (build) in Scotland.

5 Use one of the conditional link words below to complete sentences 1–6. Use each link word once only.

as long as   provided   supposing
even if   unless   if

1 _____ you had missed the train, what would you have done then?

2 I don't think you should dye your hair blue _____ you really want to upset your parents.

3 We'll never get there by lunch-time _____ we leave at ten o'clock.

4 _____ you let me know what you would like to eat, I'll do the cooking.

5 You can go to the party _____ you don't come home alone.

6 I wouldn't wear that dress to an interview _____ I were you.

Let's Get Organized

Reading

1 Skim read the article below, ignoring the missing paragraphs. What is the main issue discussed in the article? Choose a, b, or c.

   a how to cut down the amount of rubbish we produce

   b how to reduce the cost of rubbish disposal

   c how to encourage people to recycle rubbish

2 Now read paragraphs A–G. Six of these paragraphs fit into the gaps in the article. There is one extra paragraph which doesn't fit anywhere. Insert the paragraphs into gaps 1–6. Remember to look for linking devices.

Garbage in, Garbage out

Some rituals of modern domestic living vary little throughout the developed world. One such is the municipal refuse collection: usually once a week, your rubbish bags or the contents of your bin disappear into the bowels of a special lorry and are carted away to the local tip.

(1)____

Yet the marginal cost of rubbish disposal is not zero at all. The more people throw away, the more rubbish collectors and trucks are needed, and the more the local council has to pay in landfill and tipping fees.

(2)____

But as Don Fullerton and Thomas Kinnaman, two American economists, have found, this seemingly easy application of economic sense to an everyday problem has surprisingly intricate and sometimes disappointing results.

(3)____

In the paper published last year Messrs Fullerton and Kinnaman studied the effects of one such scheme, introduced in July 1992 in Charlottesville, Virginia, a town of about 40,000 people. Residents were charged 80 cents for each sticker. This may sound like the sensible use of market forces. In fact, the authors conclude, the scheme's benefits did not cover the cost of printing stickers, the sticker-sellers' commissions, and the wages of the people running the scheme.

(4)____

This is inefficient: compacting is done better by machines at landfill sites than by individuals, however enthusiastically. The weight of rubbish collected in Charlottesville (a better indicator of disposal costs than volume) fell by a modest 14%.

(5)____

The one bright spot in all this seems to have been a 15% increase in the weight of materials recycled, suggesting that people chose to recycle free rather than pay to have their refuse carted away. But the fee may have little to do with the growth in recycling, as many citizens were already participating in Charlottesville's voluntary recycling scheme.

(6)____

Intricate economic models are often needed to sort them out. And sometimes, the results of this rummaging do not smell sweet.

A

True, the number of bags or cans collected did fall sharply, by 37% between May and September 1992. But rather than buy more tags, people simply crammed more garbage – about 40% more – into each container.

B

This looks like the most basic of economic misunderstandings: if rubbish disposal is free, people will produce too much rubbish. The obvious economic solution is to make households pay the marginal cost of disposing of their waste. That will give them an incentive to throw out less and recycle more.

C

In the past few years several American towns and cities have started charging households for generating rubbish. The commonest system is to sell stickers or tags which householders attach to rubbish bags or cans. Only bags with these labels are picked up in the weekly collection.

D

It would be foolish to generalize from this one case, but the moral is clear: economic incentives sometimes produce unforeseen responses. To discourage dumping, for instance, local councils might have to spend more on catching litterers, or raise fines for littering, or cut the price of legitimate rubbish collection.

E

Less pleasing still, some people resorted to illegal dumping rather than pay to have their rubbish removed. This is hard to measure directly. But the authors, observing that a few households in the sample stopped putting rubbish out, guess that illegal dumping may account for 30 – 40% of the reduction in collected rubbish.

F

Does all this mean that the idea of charging households for the rubbish they generate is daft? Not at all: free disposal, after all, is surely too cheap. But the effects of seemingly simple policies are often complex.

G

To economists, this ceremony is peculiar, because in most places it is free. Yes, households pay for the service out of local taxes. But at the margin the price is zero: the family that fills four bins with rubbish each week pays no more than the elderly couple that fills one.

Vocabulary

1 In the article above you came across the words *inefficient* and *misunderstanding*. How do the prefixes, *in-* and *mis-*, change the meaning of these words?

2 From the list below choose the words which can combine with either *in* or *mis*.

experience	print
interpretation	management
fortune	treated
convenience	competent
correct	definite

3 Complete the sentences below with an appropriate word from the list with its correct prefix.

1 The guarantee does not cover damage resulting from _____ use.

2 The parcel was not delivered on time and this caused me great _____.

3 As a direct result of the director's _____ the company went bankrupt.

4 Because the memo was unclear it was open to _____.

5 Tom was criticised for his _____ handling of the problem.

6 I noticed a _____ when I was reading through the article.

7 They had the _____ to be hit by a severe storm.

8 The manager is away for an _____ period.

9 He hadn't been driving very long so the accident was largely due to his _____.

10 The workers went on strike because one of their colleagues was being _____.

English in Use

Part 6

1 Read the following extract from an article about moving house, ignoring the spaces. Moving house is a particularly stressful event. What does the article suggest you should do to minimize stress?

2 Now read the article again and choose the best phrase given on the right it to fill in each of the blanks. Write one letter (A–K) in the blank. Some of the suggested answers do not fit at all. The exercise begins with an example.

A   Arrange your moving date

B   Hassle can be avoided

C   With moving house

D   It's worth asking the removal company

E   The removals firm will provide

F   You should get cost quotations

G   If you pack yourself

H   If you are concerned

I   So this means that forward planning

J   You will probably be expected

K   The first, and most important, step

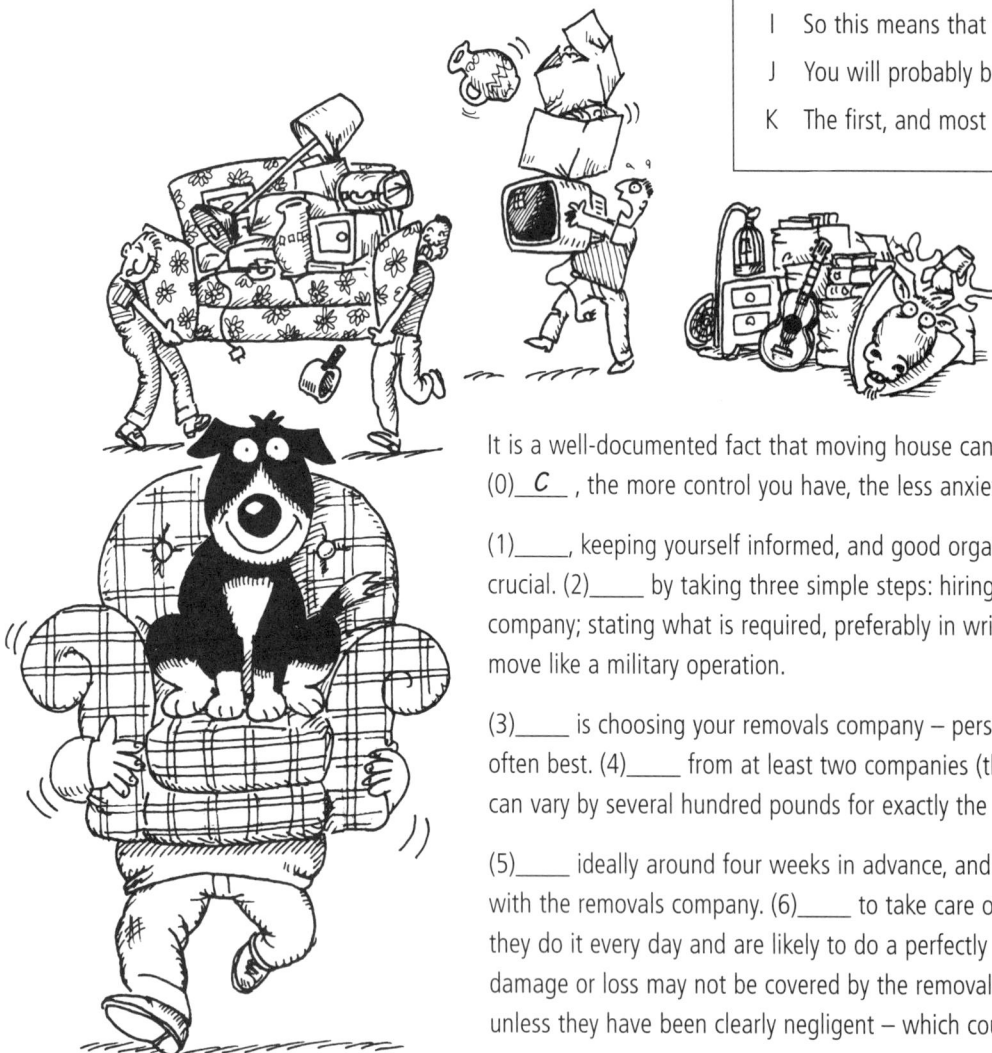

It is a well-documented fact that moving house can be a stressful event. (0) __C__ , the more control you have, the less anxiety you will experience.

(1)_____, keeping yourself informed, and good organization are absolutely crucial. (2)_____ by taking three simple steps: hiring a reputable moving company; stating what is required, preferably in writing; and planning your move like a military operation.

(3)_____ is choosing your removals company – personal recommendation is often best. (4)_____ from at least two companies (they should be free). Prices can vary by several hundred pounds for exactly the same job.

(5)_____ ideally around four weeks in advance, and confirm this in writing with the removals company. (6)_____ to take care of the packing. After all, they do it every day and are likely to do a perfectly decent job. (7)_____ any damage or loss may not be covered by the removal company's insurance unless they have been clearly negligent – which could be hard to prove.

Making All The Right Moves

Writing

1 Read the task below. What would you hope to achieve by writing such a letter?

> You have recently moved house. During the move several items were broken and you know that the removals firm were responsible. Although you have spoken to the company they have not got back to you and it is now several weeks since the move.
>
> You have the company's written guarantee of satisfaction for their work to refer to. Write a letter of complaint to the company.

2 Read through the opening paragraph, which has been done for you. What is the purpose of this paragraph?

3 Complete the letter of complaint remembering to include:

a reference to the company's 'guarantee of satisfaction'

b what items were damaged

c how much it will cost to replace them

d what action you wish them to take

The letter should be about 200 words in total. You may find it useful to refer to the Vocabulary Resource (5.1–5.5).

12 Oak Tree Lane
Godmanchester
GM2 46L

9 February 1999
Your reference:

Dear Sir

On the 12 December 1998 your company moved the contents of my house from 35 George Street, Godmanchester to the above address. During the move several items were damaged. As soon as your employees discovered the damage they reported this to me and they agreed that damage had been caused by a table inside the van which had broken loose during the journey. They admitted that the table could not have been securely fastened. As I have heard nothing from you since reporting the damage …

English in Use

Part 1

1 Read the article below, ignoring the spaces, and decide on the title.

a   Mission Impossible

b   Household Management

c   Grand Strategy

"**Every** head of household should strive to be cheerful, and should never fail to show a deep interest in the well-being of those who claim the protection of her roof." Thus spoke Isabella Beeton, whose pioneering "Book of Household Management" (0)_____ generations of women how to run the not-for-profit small businesses that were Victorian homes.

Published in 1861 when she was in her early twenties, the book was a (1)_____ best-seller: 60,000 copies sold in its first year. But Mrs Beeton had not learnt her management (2)_____ in large corporations. Stephen Covey, a successful management guru, already has a best-seller to his (3)_____: his tome on "The 7 habits of Highly Effective People" has sold 7m copies. Now, going one better than Mrs Beeton, he has just published a book on "The 7 Habits of Highly Effective Families" which applies (4)_____ of good corporate management to, as the sub-title puts it, "building a beautiful family culture in a turbulent world".

Mr Covey (5)_____ the family (he is in the 19th century league, with nine children); Mrs Beeton was mainly concerned with rules for organizing the 5 to 35 full-time resident employees that her readers would (6)_____ have had to deploy. Both stress the need for clear guidance. "To have a sense of (7)_____ is one of the most effective things a family can accomplish," says Mr Covey. He is (8)_____ on family mission statements and regular meetings to discuss its common (9)_____.

Other management experts see ways to (10)_____ the rules of the boardroom in the kitchen. "Men tend to (11)_____ as non-executive chairman in the home," says Cary Cooper of the University of Manchester Institute of Science and Technology. "Women usually carry out the human resources management (12)_____."

But most management gurus are male. Perhaps it is time for another Mrs Beeton to (13)_____ the principles learnt in the home to the corporate world. Robin Wensley, a management professor who has analysed Mrs Beeton's approach, points out that her emphasis was on (14)_____ operational control. The grand questions of strategy that (15)_____ most gurus are, he says, often irrelevant for corporate managers. As Mrs Beeton nearly said, "First, catch your hare."

⏱ **350 words**

2 Read the article again carefully and underline the words in 1–15 which best fit each space. The first one has been done for you as an example.

0 A disciplined B <u>taught</u> C coached D presented
1 A runaway B runner C running D rundown
2 A manners B facilities C techniques D procedures
3 A title B honour C fame D name
4 A beliefs B principles C laws D codes
5 A emphasizes B focuses C impresses D strengthens
6 A essentially B characteristically C conventionally D typically
7 A aim B intention C purpose D point
8 A enthusiastic B intense C forceful D keen
9 A objects B goals C ambitions D ends
10 A apply B try C fit D practise
11 A manage B operate C work D play
12 A business B job C duty D function
13 A continue B extend C increase D reach
14 A accurate B definite C precise D exact
15 A prepare B prescribe C preserve D preoccupy

Structure

1 Rewrite the following sentences in the passive. One sentence cannot be changed. Explain why you would use this form in each rewritten sentence by referring to the explanations a–c given on page 158 of the Student's Book.

1 You press the button on the left to turn the air-conditioning on.

2 The human resources manager informed the staff of the need for redundancies.

3 The post office sent the letter to the wrong address.

4 They are going to replace all the windows in the apartment block with sealed units.

5 A small company in the west of England make this solid wood furniture.

6 The seminar participants gave all the teachers a small gift at the end of the day.

7 Nobody has seen the document yet.

8 A committee will look into the matter.

9 She treated herself to a new computer.

10 They claim that the Government is on the brink of defeat.

2 Complete the following sentences with an appropriate form of *have (something done)* and the words in brackets. The first one has been done for you as an example.

0 Your garden is a mess. You really should __*have it cleared*__ (clear).

1 My car broke down yesterday. I went to the garage _____ (fix).

2 My hair looks dreadful today! I _____ _____ (only/cut last week).

3 While we are away I _____ _____ (house/paint).

4 Could you arrange _____ _____ (dog/vaccinate)?

5 Before the meeting starts make sure that _____ (coffee/order).

6 The man was interviewed by the police and then _____ (fingerprints/take).

7 Because it's so dark in my office I _____ _____ (extra lighting/put in).

8 While he was waiting for the taxi he _____ _____ (luggage/steal).

13 Law and Order

Reading

1 Read through the article quickly, ignoring the questions. Which of the headlines below is the most appropriate?

Six month sentence for juror

When a juror's the accused

Judge stands up for juror's personal beliefs

Jurors fail to agree so Judge decides

2 Read the article again carefully and then answer the multiple-choice questions.

Laura Kriho held out against a guilty verdict in a drugs trial and found herself in the dock and facing a fine.

Christopher Reed on a case troubling the US judicial system

The trial and conviction of Laura Kriho, a juror whose views put her in the dock, have become an issue pitting an increasingly authoritarian
5 US judicial system against a people's jury movement.

Kriho, is appealing against her conviction and a $1,200 fine for contempt of court. On the grounds of
10 her personal beliefs, she was the lone hold-out among 12 jurors in a trial of a woman charged with possessing amphetamines. In Britain, where a majority verdict secures a conviction,
15 her stance would pass unnoticed. But in America, where all but two states require a unanimous verdict, the growing movement of "jury nullification" is causing grave
20 concern.

In punishing Kriho, Judge Henry Nieto appears to have invented a new crime: "failing as a potential juror to disclose information the court would
25 like to have heard". The concept of "jury nullification" so scares the US legal establishment that Judge Nieto formally denied it in his ruling; deciding instead that she "obstructed
30 justice".

Nullification is a right dating back to 17th century England, when a London jury refused to convict the Quaker William Penn (who later
35 founded Pennsylvania) of preaching to an unlawful assembly.

Since then, juries in both countries have been able to ignore a judge's directions and vote according to their
40 consciences, even if this goes against

the evidence. But in the US, courts are prevented from informing jurors of this right under a Supreme Court ruling in the 1890s.
45 In Britain juries are sworn "to give a true verdict according to the evidence", but jurors in several high-profile cases have brought in "perverse" verdicts against the weight
50 of the evidence to reflect their disapproval of the prosecution.

In the case in which Kriho sat as a juror last year, the panel divided 11–1 and a mistrial was declared. But Judge
55 Kenneth Barnhill became suspicious when the jury passed out a note asking if a juror could be dismissed for looking up the sentence for drug possession on the Internet, something
60 Kriho acknowledged she had done.

The judge thought he recognized the imprint of the Fully Informed Jury Association (the FIJA), a nation-wide movement of libertarians who are pushing for juries to exercise their right to veto the law. Kriho knew about FIJA and believed that minor drug offences did not belong in a courtroom. Her views have made her yet another fallen soldier in America's long war on drugs.

Judge Barnhill issued contempt of court charges against her. Her fellow jurors were forced to give evidence about their arguments with her, thus breaking the promise that jury room deliberations are forever secret.

Four months later, Judge Nieto issued his ruling, dismissing two of the contempt charges and declining to imprison her, although she faced a maximum sentence of six months. Kriho's lawyer, Paul Grant, told the judge: "The court is trying to intimidate anybody with an independent mind. The government cannot tell its citizens to think critically of the law or the government."

Grant condemns the Nieto ruling as "dangerous" because it threatens every juror with criminal prosecution "for not volunteering what they were not specifically asked". What this conviction establishes is that courts can exclude from the jury any juror who understands the historical rights of jurors, and any juror who thinks critically of the government and its laws, or who reserves an independence of mind to determine what would constitute a just verdict.

It is well known that both sides use the US "voir dire" process, in which jurors are asked their opinions, often on personal matters, to exclude anyone with forceful opinions or extra knowledge of the case and its political or social context. A powerful campaign exists in America to limit jury powers further, ending the present system by exchanging ordinary citizens for retired lawyers and judges.

The Kriho case is crucial to this debate. It is the first time in US history that a juror in a criminal case has been tried and convicted for telling fellow jurors they have the right to acquit, even if they believe the accused broke the law.

Some judges have denounced FIJA's aims as a "return to anarchy". But an editorial in the American Bar Association's Litigation journal supports a proposed law in Missouri to compel judges to inform jurors of their rights. "A clear and adequate instruction could be conveyed in a single sentence," it says, "explaining that the jury should (not 'must') convict anyone proven guilty beyond a reasonable doubt, unless the jurors have a firm belief that a conviction would be fundamentally unjust." That seems simple enough, but Grant believes he may have to go to the Supreme Court for a final ruling.

810 words

1 How did Laura Kriho upset the US judicial system?

  A She did not agree with her fellow jurors.

  B She would not pay her $1000 fine.

  C She joined a people's jury movement.

  D She objected to the unanimous verdict requirement.

2 Why did Judge Nieto invent a new crime?

  A He wanted to remove Kriho from the jury.

  B He believed that Kriho was a weak juror.

  C He wanted to avoid references to 'jury nullification'.

  D He believed that Kriho was involved in a crime.

3 Why have some jurors in Britain refused to convict in certain cases?

  A They did not think the evidence was strong enough.

  B They wanted to express dissatisfaction with the prosecution.

  C They believed that the accused were innocent.

  D They knew they did not have to agree with the judge.

4 What was Judge Barnhill suspicious about?

  A He thought the jury was acting illegally.

  B He believed that Kriho was a drug user.

  C He thought that other jurors were being threatened.

  D He believed that Kriho was involved with the FIJA.

5 Why did Kriho's lawyer think Judge Nieto's ruling was dangerous?

  A It will encourage jurors to break the law.

  B It will give the courts too much power.

  C It will allow jurors to express extreme views.

  D It will make jury selection more difficult.

6 The aim of the FIJA is to make the American people aware that they

  A do not need to accept a judge's ruling.

  B have a right to change unfair laws.

  C do not have to reveal what is said in the jury room.

  D do not have to stand down from a jury when requested.

Vocabulary

1 In the article you came across the following phrasal verbs. Look back at the verbs in context. Can you explain what they mean?

    a held out (line 11)

    b passed out (line 56)

    c looking up (line 58)

2 All these verbs have more than one meaning. Do you know any other meanings?

3 Now select one of the verbs for each of the sentences below.

    1 The pain was so intense that he _____ and had to be carried off the pitch.

    2 We can stay here for as long as our food supplies _____.

    3 Why don't you _____ the word in a dictionary if you want to check the spelling.

    4 I'm not _____ on you. I really don't know where he is.

    5 The forthcoming talks _____ a real possibility of peace between the two sides.

    6 She _____ from her book as I entered the room.

    7 Things are really beginning to _____ since she got that new job.

Writing

1 Read the task below. What sort of person do you think the family is looking for?

> Someone you know well wants to spend a year with a family in a Spanish-speaking country in order to improve their Spanish whilst helping the family with their children and doing some jobs in the house to help the parents. You have been asked by the family to write a reference for him. You should write a detailed reference saying how you know this person and for how long. You should describe their strengths and weaknesses and say why you would support their application.

2 Read the following sentences which will form the first two paragraphs of the reference and put them into an appropriate order.

    1 I taught Jason throughout that time and also got to know him well outside school as he attended the youth club which I help to run.

    2 In his final year he not only performed in but also directed the end-of-term production of 'A Midsummer Night's Dream'.

    3 Jason was also an enthusiastic and regular member of the youth club.

    4 I was very impressed by his ability to encourage and control younger pupils.

    5 I was always able to rely on him to help me organize activities for the other members.

    6 He was particularly keen on drama and appeared in several school plays.

    7 In school, Jason was a hard-working and lively student.

    8 He did particularly well in Spanish in his final exams and I know he would like to spend some time in Spain to improve further.

    9 I am a teacher at the Bowland Secondary School in Blackburn, Lancashire, where Jason Cooper has been a pupil for the last five years.

3 Now complete the reference in about 125 words. Remember to mention:

    a any possible weaknesses in his personality.

    b why you think he would be suitable for the work.

English in Use

Part 5

1 Read this informal e-mail message to a work colleague. What is the aim of the message?

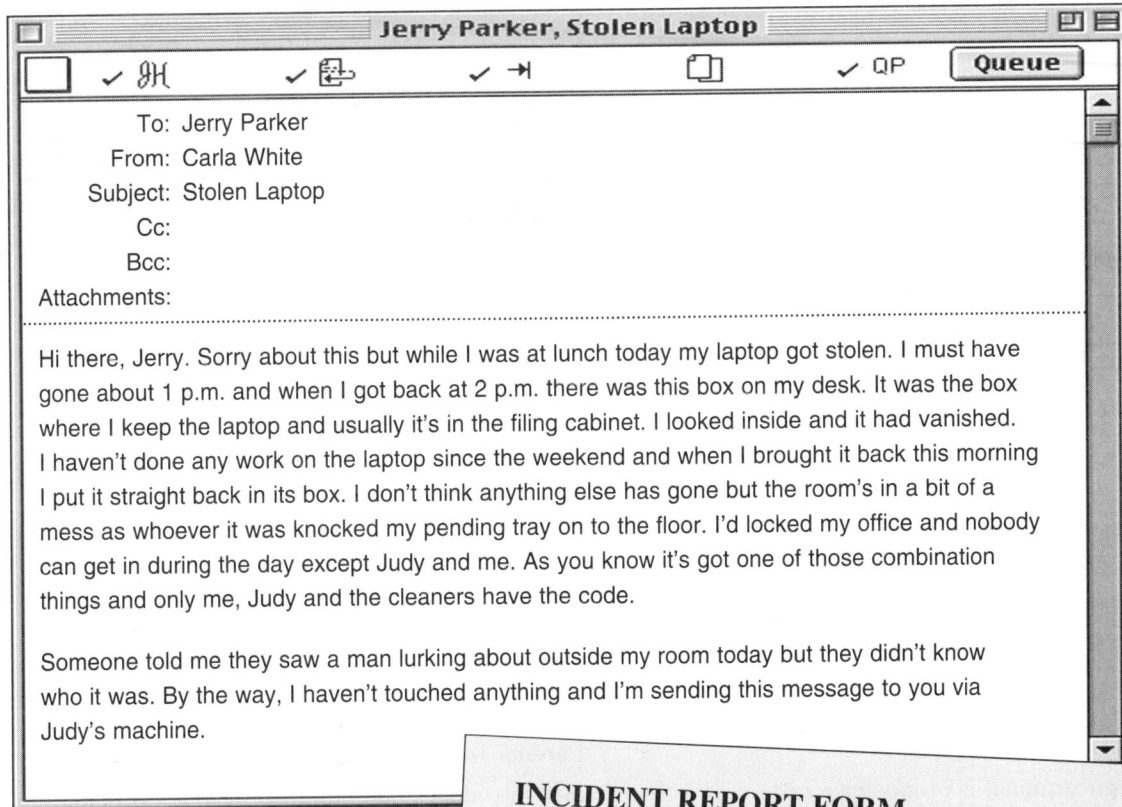

```
┌─────────────────────────────────────────────────────────────┐
│ ▭ ▭▭▭▭▭      Jerry Parker, Stolen Laptop      ▭▭▭▭  ⊟⊞ │
├─────────────────────────────────────────────────────────────┤
│  ☐  ✓ ℐℋ    ✓ 🔁    ✓ ⇥    ⬚    ✓ QP   [ Queue ] │
├─────────────────────────────────────────────────────────────┤
│         To: Jerry Parker                                  ▲ │
│       From: Carla White                                   ▒ │
│    Subject: Stolen Laptop                                    │
│         Cc:                                                  │
│        Bcc:                                                  │
│  Attachments:                                               │
│ ............................................................│
│  Hi there, Jerry. Sorry about this but while I was at lunch  │
│  today my laptop got stolen. I must have gone about 1 p.m.  │
│  and when I got back at 2 p.m. there was this box on my     │
│  desk. It was the box where I keep the laptop and usually   │
│  it's in the filing cabinet. I looked inside and it had     │
│  vanished. I haven't done any work on the laptop since the  │
│  weekend and when I brought it back this morning I put it   │
│  straight back in its box. I don't think anything else has  │
│  gone but the room's in a bit of a mess as whoever it was   │
│  knocked my pending tray on to the floor. I'd locked my     │
│  office and nobody can get in during the day except Judy    │
│  and me. As you know it's got one of those combination      │
│  things and only me, Judy and the cleaners have the code.   │
│                                                             │
│  Someone told me they saw a man lurking about outside my    │
│  room today but they didn't know who it was. By the way, I  │
│  haven't touched anything and I'm sending this message to   │
│  you via Judy's machine.                                  ▼ │
└─────────────────────────────────────────────────────────────┘
```

2 Using the information in the note, complete the formal report using no more than two words in each gap.
Remember:

a check the register of the report you are completing.

b make sure that the words you use do not occur in the informal e-mail message.

c read through your completed report to make sure that the style is consistent.

INCIDENT REPORT FORM

Name: Carla White

Division: International Development

Type of Incident: Theft of Laptop

Date and time of incident: Monday, 3 February, 1–2 p.m.

Description of Incident:

I left the office at 1 p.m. and on (0) _**my return**_ at 2 p.m. I noticed the box where I store my laptop computer was on the desk. It is normally kept in the filing cabinet. I looked inside the box and the laptop (1)_____ . The laptop was (2)_____ at the weekend and I (3)_____ it to the office this morning. There does not (4)_____ to be anything else missing although my pending tray had (5)_____ on to the floor. The door to the office was locked and nobody has (6)_____ to the room in office hours apart from Judy Oldham, my secretary, and myself. You are probably (7)_____ that there is a combination security lock on the door. The code to the lock is only (8) _____ Ms Oldham, the cleaning (9)_____ and myself.

It has been (10)_____ to me that a man was seen in (11)_____ during the morning but (12)_____ was unknown.

Nothing has been touched since the incident and messages etc. have been sent via Ms Oldham's computer.

English in Use

Part 2

1 Read the following article about youth crime, ignoring the spaces. What is the writer's opinion of the measures the government is proposing? What reasons does the writer give?

2 Read the article again and supply the missing words by writing one word in spaces 1–15. The first one has been done for you as an example.

Nobody denies that youth crime is a problem. (0)___*According*___ to government surveys, one quarter of boys under the age of 18 and a fifth of girls in the same age group have committed a crime, and a quarter of (1)_____ known offenders are under 18. Not only has youth crime risen by 40% (2)_____ the last decade, (3)_____ the number of young offenders brought to court has fallen by the same proportion. The police solve only 5% of (4)_____ offences, and only 3% of offences result in a charge or caution.

So the government is proposing a raft (5)_____ reforms of the police, social services and youth courts to rein in young criminals. New "youth-offender teams" will bring (6)_____ police, probation officers, court officials, local schools and parents to devise action plans in individual cases.

The youth-offender teams would supervize a range of new punishments, (7)_____ reparation orders, obliging children to confront the victims of their crimes (8)_____ to perform community service in recompense.

But pressure has driven the government to embellish sensible proposals (9)_____

several crowd-pleasing punitive methods that are now destined to become law. The new Crime and Disorder Bill will give local authorities the power to set curfews for young people (10)_____ an effort to crack down on gangs. Civil liberties groups object to (11)_____ a wholesale attack on freedom of movement, claiming that it might actually increase offending (12)_____ criminalizing millions of otherwise law-abiding children.

Parents are not safe (13)_____: the Bill also introduces parental responsibility orders, which would allow the courts to force parents to control their children. The government admits that few parents wilfully disregard their children's behaviour. Its plans for youth crime teams suggest that, by failing to provide co-ordinated support from all government agencies, the current system is letting parents down – (14)_____ the other way round. (15)_____ the responsibility order shifts the blame back on to parents. It would be a shame if populist pressures force the government to undermine their own improvements to the youth justice system.

Structure

1 Find an example of an inversion in the article opposite.

2 Complete sentences 1–8 with a suitable subject/verb inversion:

1 No longer _____
responsibility for their children.

2 In no way _____
_____ to roam the streets at night.

3 Only when the police and other agencies
co-ordinate their activities _____
a decrease in the crime figures.

4 Rarely _____ such interest
in the causes of youth crime.

5 Not only _____
crimes but many girls are involved as well.

6 Only by insisting on a curfew _____
_____ to a minimum.

7 Never before _____
_____ to such an extent
in the lives of young people.

8 Not until _____
_____ safer places to live and work.

3 Find two examples of concessions in the article at the beginning of this unit.

4 Combine the information in 1–8 with that in a–h using the following expressions at least once.

in spite of   although   despite   not that
even though   even if

1 there were more police on the streets
2 he had a good education
3 having spent many years in prison
4 She has had little experience of dealing with offenders
5 They were desperate to visit him
6 the serious nature of the case
7 The children refused to go with the social worker
8 the number of patients that day

a that should mean she can't learn how to
b the judge let him go with just a caution
c the doctor was able to visit the old man that evening
d it meant they had to go home alone
e he wasn't able to get a job
f it wouldn't prevent crime
g he did not bear a grudge against society
h it meant a long and difficult journey

5 Complete sentences 1–8 in any way you think suitable.

1 Even though …, I am not going to … .
2 There have been a lot of break-ins round here lately – not that … .
3 Despite …, he was not convicted of the crime.
4 I would like to move out of the area except that … .
5 While Barry was reasonably intelligent, he … .
6 For most children praise from adults is very important, whereas … .
7 Much as we would like to agree with you, … .
8 In spite of …, the judge decided … .

Tomorrow's World

English in Use

Part 1

Read this article about robot football and choose the best word, A, B, C or D, to fill in the spaces. An example is given.

SILICON SOCCER

In a tense final that went to extra time, America (0)_____ Japan in Nagoya, and took the 1997 Robocup. This was the first ever World Cup for robots, with eight (1)_____ in the 'Under 50cm diameter' class battling it (2)_____. Matches are short: two five-minute halves divided by a 10-minute break, when the robots' builders bring on refreshments in the (3)_____ of a battery recharge.

The whole event is in fact a showcase for an (4)_____ electronic technology that is going to have a major (5)_____ on our lives. Robots are programmed in teams to accomplish complicated and dangerous tasks, such as repairing a nuclear reactor or (6)_____ landmines. Instead of passing balls to each other, today's football team could be rolling rocks around planets tomorrow.

According to Robocup (7)_____, every 'player' must function independently, using only its own programming and information (8)_____ by radio from its 'team-mates'. Most teams choose to transmit visual images to the robots from a video camera suspended over the 'pitch', but the Japanese have fixed mini cameras onto the robots themselves. (9)_____, because of the miniaturization, their view is much more limited, which (10)_____ gave them a disadvantage in the final.

The Americans – 'Team Newton', from Newton Labs in Seattle – triumphed because of their superior overhead vision and decision-making system. This (11)_____ the incoming data, took speed measurements 250 times every second, and then, like a chess computer, plotted hundreds of simple situations. In this way, the Newton robots were 'coached' more effectively and (12)_____ to be tough opposition from the outset. In the smaller 'Under 15cm class', the French were the only team to score a goal against them. Indeed, the French might have done better still, if they hadn't (13)_____ played the Spanish: it turned out that both sides were using the same radio frequency to (14)_____ their robots. This inevitably resulted in total confusion, with the match being abandoned as a no-score draw. Just (15)_____ what would happen if Atletico Madrid and Aston Villa were to go out wearing the same strip!

360 words

0	A <u>beat</u>	B won	C gained	D hit
1	A candidates	B contestants	C competitors	D champions
2	A on	B up	C down	D out
3	A manner	B form	C place	D kind
4	A emerging	B appearing	C issuing	D arising
5	A jolt	B impact	C blow	D contact
6	A disposing	B disbanding	C dismantling	D disusing
7	A penalties	B laws	C sentences	D rules
8	A relayed	B replaced	C reviewed	D released
9	A However	B Although	C Despite	D Whereas
10	A unsuccessfully	B unbelievably	C undoubtedly	D unwillingly
11	A worked	B analysed	C experimented	D dissolved
12	A proved	B showed	C revealed	D justified
13	A virtually	B eventually	C actually	D marginally
14	A command	B advance	C control	D lead
15	A believe	B assume	C dream	D imagine

Reading

1 Skim read the article about urban planning. According to Stephen Graham, is there a future for the world's cities?

2 Now read the article again and identify the paragraphs which answer the following questions.

Which paragraph (A–K) talks about:

the drawbacks of telecommuting	1 ___
new economic infrastructures in cities	2 ___
the argument that cities cannot survive	3 ___
traditional urban problems	4 ___
new methods adopted by urban planners	5 ___
the relocation of parts of some businesses	6 ___
new problems faced by planners	7 ___
current use of the Internet	8 ___
how cities relate to electronic activity	9 ___

3 Find the following words and phrases in the article. Check you understand their meaning, by looking at the surrounding context. Line numbers are given in brackets.

a bombarded (1)	i arbitrary (56)
b undermined (9)	j burgeoning (57)
c bound up by (24)	k smart (70)
d stem from (25)	l rapid transit (74)
e feed off (32)	m integrated (75)
f counter-intuitive (36)	n influx (92)
g powerhouses (44)	o volatile (103)
h once-defined (56)	p fragmented (103)

4 In 3f, the prefix *counter-* appeared. This prefix combines with words to make new words with an opposite meaning. So, the verb *counteract* means act against, as in the following example.

The doctor gave her an injection to counteract the poison from the snakebite.

What parts of speech are these words? Check them in a dictionary if you're not sure of their meanings.

counterargument   counterbalance
counter-espionage   counter-offensive
counterpart   counter-revolutionary
counter-productive   countersign

Urban planning

by Stephen Graham

A **W**e are bombarded almost daily with excited commentary from the media, technology industries and futurists, who say that our economy, society and culture are
5 simultaneously becoming more global and shifting 'on-line'. Anything can now be done anywhere and at any time, via wires or satellites. Following on from this, the rhetoric commonly announces that the notion of the city is being undermined. Workers have started to decentralize to
10 idyllic 'electronic cottages', from where they can, remotely, maintain contact with work, family, friends and services. The days of the city are numbered. Or are they?

B Planners dismiss forecasts about the imminent 'death of cities', seeing them as both misleading and dangerously
15 simplistic. The familiar life of towns and cities will not die out just because IT capabilities are growing; a lot more holds urban developments together and sustains their growth than their ability to support concentrated, face-to-face communication.

C In fact, the urban dominance of our economy, society and culture shows few signs of waning. With the emergence of 'mega-cities', global urban dominance is growing rapidly. What is changing is that cities are becoming more and more bound up by IT networks in all aspects of life. This
25 means that the classic planning issues that stem from concentrated living in urban areas – physical development, traffic congestion, pollution, environmental conflict, and social and cultural divisions and inequalities – will continue to fill planners' in-trays.

D Rather than being replaced, transport demands are rising in parallel with the exploding use of telecommunications. Both feed off each other in complex ways, and the shift is towards a highly mobile and communications-intensive society. The links between interaction in urban places and
35 'electronic spaces' are therefore complex, subtle, and sometimes counter-intuitive. In the City of London, for example, highly concentrated growth continues, fuelled by the need for more face-to-face contact in order to interpret the huge flows of information on global IT networks.

E 'Cities reflect the economic realities of the 21st century,' writes Tony Fitzpatrick, the Director of Ove Arup, a leading architectural consultancy and construction company. 'Remote working from self-sufficient farmsteads via the Internet cannot replace the powerhouses of personal

45 interaction, which drives teamwork and creativity. Besides, you cannot look into someone's eyes and see that they are trustworthy over the Internet.'

F In the USA, the Internet is actually growing faster in the biggest urban areas, quite disproportionately to the country
50 as a whole. This demonstrates that it is the very activities of information-producing cities which have been driving the growth of the Internet in the last three years.

G That said, planners still confront some uneasy dilemmas. First, what is to become of urban and regional planning
55 policies aimed at particular geographical areas, now that these once-defined spaces start to appear arbitrary, within the burgeoning world of electronic information flow and interconnection. Second, how can strategies be developed that position individual places favourably within the
60 'information society', when few planners have any knowledge of, or power over, information infrastructures and the complex social processes through which they are applied and used? Does all this mean that planners must get involved in this strange new world?

H Many local planning agencies are already beginning to experiment with information infrastructures as planning tools to help shape new types of urban places, in what may be termed urban 'tele-planning' initiatives. Examples of this can be drawn from all over the world. In California, new
70 urban 'tele-village' or 'smart community' initiatives are widespread, with the attempt to insert fibre-optic grids and advanced information services into the fabric of relatively high-density communities. In Los Angeles, urban tele-villages are being positioned near rapid transit stations,

75 within ambitious, integrated plans to manage transport and teleworking together in the effort to reduce the use of cars.

I Most large, dynamic cities already have their campus-like 'technopoles', usually in green areas, which house science parks, corporate research and development centres, and
80 university business schools. Cities like Lille, Cologne and Sunderland have gone further, developing high-profile 'teleports' which connect local industries directly to advanced services and satellite ground stations.

J Transnational companies are choosing to locate their 'data-
85 crunching' and customer support operations in countries such as India, Jamaica and the Philippines, creating yet more complex networked urban geographies, strung out across the world. The city of Bangalore, known as India's Silicon Valley, is seeing a new cycle of frantic urbanization,
90 fuelled by the influx of global technology firms eager to access the cheap, highly skilled professionals who are available there.

K The shift to a globally interconnected 'network society' requires particular urban places within which the intense
95 face-to-face demands of the world of work, along with cultural, leisure and social activities, can be met effectively and productively. It is not therefore surprising that 'tele-planning' is emerging as a central strand of planning practice. Cities are fast becoming extended urban regions,
100 rather than monocentric urban cores, and are without doubt the key anchor points in today's volatile and fragmented world.

🕐 **850 words**

English in Use

Part 4

Read this article about plastic loyalty cards and their role in shopping. Then look at gaps 1–8 and decide what part of speech is required in each. Make suitable words from the ones given in capital letters, remembering to add negative prefixes where necessary.

0	RESPONSIBLE	5	ANALYSE
1	ACCUMULATE	6	RESPOND
2	APPEAR	7	PART
3	INFORM	8	PERSON
4	EXPLAIN		

Aiming to serve

Writing the shopping list is almost as tedious a (0) **responsibility** as trekking round the supermarket, and it would be a huge benefit if the store could do this for you. That day cannot be far off, thanks to the massive (1)_____ of data on millions of customers who already use so-called loyalty cards. Loyalty has nothing to do with it – at least, not yet – as is all too (2)_____ from the many people who hold every supermarket card there is.

Why then are supermarkets so keen to issue these cards? The answer is that in a technologically-sophisticated world, they provide highly (3)_____ data about customers and their shopping habits. One US chain noticed that Friday nights saw a seemingly

(4)_____ peak in purchases of both baby's nappies and alcohol. In their subsequent (5)_____ of the sales data, they concluded that men were being sent out for emergency baby supplies and were seizing the opportunity to stock up on beer at the same time. Their immediate (6)_____ was to place the nappies closer to the beer!

This is all part of the move away from mass marketing in favour of its newly-heralded (7)_____, 'micro marketing'. Supermarkets are in essence reinventing the culture of the traditional corner shop, by calling on this new-found, (8)_____ knowledge of their customers.

Structure

1 Read what a French technician at the Robocup event said. Then report his words, remembering to make it clear who he is referring to throughout.

> " The American team is very strong and we knew at the start of this competition that they would be hard to beat. In the Under 15 centimetre class, we are in fact the only team who have managed to score against them. Our performance at this year's event has been good, on the whole. The one disaster, of course, was our match against the Spanish. It is an amazing coincidence that my Spanish counterpart and I selected the same radio frequency! Still, at least we didn't lose the match. "

2 Match the two halves of the sentences below, adding a suitable conjunction from the ones given.

although   as   despite   even if   so that   whereas

a   People will always want to use books

b   Endoscopic surgery is a radical development

c   The Internet offers children a huge store of information

d   Hotels catering for the business sector are forced to introduce new facilities

e   Teleworking seems to offer a more attractive lifestyle

f   There is little evidence to suggest that people shop at only one supermarket

1   the fact that pornography could also be accessed is of great concern.

2   their having a loyalty card.

3   it allows operations to be carried out by remote control.

4   in reality, many people miss the social contact of an office.

5   their clients don't choose to go elsewhere.

6   the technology to replace them is eventually perfected.

3 Read these sentence openers, correcting the word order, where necessary, to produce suitable inversions. Then complete the sentences with ideas of your own.

a   Hardly a new computer has been launched before _____

_____

b   Not only electronic mail is convenient _____

_____

_____

c   Only by conducting further research we will know for sure _____

_____

d   No longer people will have to make the trek to the local supermarket _____

_____

Writing

Read this report about telemedicine and correct any errors in punctuation.

Introduction
Telemedicine can be roughly defined, as 'medicine at a distance. It is not an entirely new phenomenon; for some time, doctors
5   have been contacting patients and colleagues by phone fax and, latterly, by e-mail. However, recent developments in communications technology have allowed this way of working to expand. The following
10   sections assess the benefits and drawbacks of telemedicine.

Teleconsulting
Through video links, it is possible for a patient to be seen by a specialist anywhere in the
15   country, while sitting in his or her local doctors surgery or hospital. One pilot scheme targeted at rural communities in Wales proved very successful, with patients and doctors alike in favour of it's continuing. Under the
20   scheme, teleconferences between doctors and patients were set up using BT's ISDN network, with additional technical support from the University of Wales.

The benefits of telemedicine
25   It is believed that telemedicine could play an important part, in reducing hospital waiting lists. A further advantage is that as teleconsultations are carried out locally with the patient's doctor on hand, there can be an
30   immediate exchange of information. This minimizes stress, since patients do not have to wait a long time to find out whether something is wrong.

Possible problems
35   As with all state-of-the-art technology, the initial investment in equipment is costly. Moreover, purchasing the equipment will not in itself guarantee success. Telemedicine is a radically, different way of working and new
40   skills have to be learned, not least in the area of communication.

Conclusion
Clearly telemedicine could be a major asset in health care of the future, though further
45   research will be needed in terms of cost, actual requirements, and its integration with existing service's.